What to do when your
parents live forever

What to do when your parents live forever

Dan and Lavinia Cohn-Sherbok

BOOKS

Winchester, U.K.
New York, U.S.A.

First published by O Books, 2007
O Books is an imprint of John Hunt Publishing Ltd.,
The Bothy, Deershot Lodge, Park Lane, Ropley, Hants, SO24 0BE, UK
office1@o-books.net
www.o-books.net

Distribution in:

UK and Europe
Orca Book Services
orders@orcabookservices.co.uk
Tel: 01202 665432
Fax: 01202 666219 Int. code (44)

USA and Canada
NBN
custserv@nbnbooks.com
Tel: 1 800 462 6420
Fax: 1 800 338 4550

Australia and New Zealand
Brumby Books
sales@brumbybooks.com.au
Tel: 61 3 9761 5535
Fax: 61 3 9761 7095

Far East (offices in Singapore, Thailand,
Hong Kong, Taiwan)
Pansing Distribution Pte Ltd
kemal@pansing.com
Tel: 65 6319 9939
Fax: 65 6462 5761

South Africa
Alternative Books
altbook@peterhyde.co.za
Tel: 021 447 5300
Fax: 021 447 1430

Text copyright Dan and Lavinia Cohn-Sherbok 2007

Design: Jim Weaver

ISBN-13: 978-1-84694-028-6
ISBN-10: 1-84694-028-1

A CIP catalogue record for this book is available from the British
Library.

Printed in the US by Maple Vail

Contents

Introduction

THE AUTHORS OF this book are part of the baby-boom generation. We were both born soon after the end of the Second World War. After the men came home from the War, women were encouraged to give up their war-time jobs to the returning soldiers. It was time to stay at home and have babies. Women married young. Ideally they were in their early twenties. If they were still single by the time they reached the great age of twenty-five, there was the dreadful fear that they would be 'on the shelf' for the rest of their lives. Families were, by today's standards, large. Three, four or even five children were not unusual. It was not only possible, but normal to buy a nice house in the suburbs with a mortgage based on the salary of one wage-earner. Every day the men went to work in their offices in the city. Meanwhile the women stayed at home and submerged themselves in homemaking and child-rearing. Feminism in those days was scarcely a gleam in Betty Friedan's eye.

Although we grew up on opposite sides of the Atlantic Ocean (Dan in Denver, Colorado, Lavinia in London, England) we had similar experiences. From an early age we both travelled to school by ourselves – the streets were thought to be safe in the late 1950s. We knew our mothers would be at home waiting for us at four o'clock. We are both old enough to remember where we were when President Kennedy was shot. We remember the excitement of the Beatles and we sung along with Bob Dylan. As part of the Swinging Sixties we were appalled that so many of our contemporaries had to fight in the Vietnam War. We sympathised with the Paris student riots of 1968. We learned to believe that we did not trust anyone over thirty and, at the same time, we both benefited hugely from the great expansion in higher education which was taking place. We were involved in feminism, in pacifism and in the summer of peace and love. And as we grew up, we continued to be part of the generation which was in the forefront of social change. After all, there were always so many of us.

We are now reaching our sixties. Having been through school, university, vocational training and many years of full-time employment, we are now beginning to think about retirement. The idea of adjusting to life without an overriding occupation should be traumatic. In fact we look forward to it. Our generation, with all its advantages, has tended to be rather good at leisure. Instead there is another deeper, darker preoccupation. We never expected it; we never asked for it and we certainly never prepared for it. What has become perhaps the most difficult and disturbing experience of our late middle age has nothing to do with our earlier preoccupations. We are, for the first time, confronted with the problem of elderly parents. Old people who show every sign of living for ever.

Life-expectancy today has dramatically increased. According to the Bible, the years of man are three-score and ten. Even though the Bible was written a long time ago, we were brought up to believe that this was about right. In the years we were growing up, men lived to be about seventy and women a few years more. To survive into the late eighties or nineties was exceptional, a feat to be admired and wondered at. Things have changed. Go into any newsagent or supermarket. Study the birthday cards. Not only are there commercial cards for the septuagenarians and octogenarians, there are special cards for those who have reached ninety and even a hundred. Again, read the obituaries in the newspapers. Some people are still dying in their sixties and seventies, but a substantial proportion are in their late eighties and nineties. No one expected that our parents would live this long, but today it seems that many of them are doing just that.

Think of the mathematics of it. Our parents' generation married young. It was normal to have babies from the early twenties onwards. Many women had finished having children by the time they were thirty. If your mother was twenty-five when you were born and she lives to be ninety-five, you will be seventy when she dies. Even if she does not quite make ninety, you will still be sixty-four. You will probably be at or near retirement. Your own health may not be as good as it was. It may be you who needs a hip replacement or a by-pass operation. Unless you have gone in for serial marriages with much younger partners, your own children will all be grown up. They will probably be parents themselves. It is no longer unusual for children to have several great-grandparents still living.

We reflect this trend in our own lives. Although Lavinia's father died of a heart attack in his late sixties, Dan's father survived until he was ninety-seven. By that time he had had two major strokes; he had survived head surgery to relieve pressure on his brain; he had also had a pacemaker fitted to stop him falling about and breaking his bones, but nothing could be done to regulate his incontinence or to revive his memory. By the end he dozed his way through his days and was recognising no one. Every winter for the last six years of his life he had pneumonia, but every year, with the aid of antibiotics, he recovered. When he finally did die, there was a general vagueness in the nursing home as to the exact cause of death. On the official certificate the doctor had written 'Cardiac Arrest', but that could apply to anyone who was dead. A more truthful explanation would have been 'Extreme Old Age.'

Both of our mothers are still alive and are in their early nineties. Dan's mother still lives in the city where she was born, Denver,

Colorado. For several years now she has had an apartment in the assisted living section of an excellent old people's residence. For the last fifteen years she has suffered from gradual macular degeneration and now she is registered blind. She also is afflicted with serious dementia and has almost no short-term memory. She still knows who we are when we telephone or visit her, but she has no recollection afterwards of these phone-calls or visits. When we are with her, she will repeat the same questions again and again. 'How old am I?', she will ask. 'You are ninety,' we say. She expresses total astonishment. And then, a minute later, she asks the same question all over again. She does not remember where we live or what we do for a living. She has even forgotten the name of her husband, although she was married to him for over sixty years and she faithfully visited him every day for the six years he was in a nursing home. She is also incontinent. Yet, despite her disabilities, she remains fundamentally in good health. She is mobile and physically quite agile. She enjoys the activities offered by the residence; she loves her food; she seems to have friends among the other old ladies (although she can neither see them nor remember their names). She is also good-tempered, docile, easy-to-deal-with and is popular with the aides who look after her. She does not seem to be unhappy.

In contrast, Lavinia's mother, who is also ninety, still lives in her own flat in London. Despite a threatened cataract, her sight is fairly good and she is fiercely independent. A few years ago she had a hip-replacement and then, a year ago, she fell and broke her other hip while getting off a bus. Even though she has made a good recovery and is mobile, she is frail and outside she walks with a stick. Sadly her hearing is very poor. She owns several hearing aids, but she hates wearing them. When the batteries wear out, she keeps them in a special tin in the vain hope that, given a short rest, they will recover their strength! After much persuasion, she has agreed to have occasional aides to help her with housework and personal care. But she is very reluctant to employ them and she sends them away on the least excuse. Increasingly she is becoming repetitive and is having trouble remembering names and faces. Often she seems confused and gives an inconsequential answer to a particular question, but this may be the result of deafness rather than dementia. In herself she is not happy. She feels isolated and lonely as almost all her friends and contemporaries have died or are beyond visiting her. She was always the centre of family life and she craves the undivided attention of her children. Sadly, her children have other commitments. She says again and again that she does not want to be a nuisance and frequently she talks about moving into an old people's home. Yet it is clear that the idea is totally repellent to her and she is in fact resisting it with all her strength. The present is not happy and the future looks even less promising.

What do you do for the best in these situations? How can you help your parents make the best of their extreme old age? What kind of feelings are you supposed to have while all this is going on? What kind of feelings do you really have? In short, what DO you do if your parents live forever? These questions haunt both of us every day. And, if you have bought this book, they no doubt trouble you as well. The purpose of this volume is to provide you with the kinds of information you need to deal with the inevitable problems that accompany old age. But it tries to go further than that. It is essentially practical and, unlike most books on the topic, it recognizes the negative feelings and the ambivalences entailed in the whole situation. Too many books on the subject pretend that there are no dilemmas and unhappinesses entailed. All that is needed is 'to do the best for Mom and Dad.' Unfortunately it is not as easy as that. There are many people involved in the equation besides ourselves and our parents. There are other siblings, children, grandchildren and other family members. There are friends, neighbours, paid help and volunteers. There are also many complicated financial difficulties. How much can be afforded? How much should be afforded? How can the money best be spent? How do we deal with the rest of the family's needs in the face of the enormous costs of geriatric care?

These are some of the questions this book is attempting to tackle. It is our aim to give the range of alternatives and to try to provide realistic solutions. Extreme old age is not easy. All we can do is to help our parents through the difficulties they must inevitably face during the final years of their lives, while, at the same time, being aware that there are other needs, equally pressing, elsewhere...

1
Growing old

EVEN AS A middle-aged person, it is not easy to perceive what our parents feel about becoming old. We live in a culture that worships youth. Everywhere the young are glamorized. Our television screens are full of exquisite young women and handsome young men. Once an actress reaches a certain age, it becomes very hard to get good parts. Even products which are designed for middle-aged people are normally advertised by models in their twenties. Everything conspires to make you believe that you must, in the words of the old song, 'Keep young and beautiful if you want to be loved.'

It is difficult enough for the middle aged to come to terms with the loss of youth and freshness. For the elderly, it is even harder. As far as the media are concerned, the old are almost invisible. Perhaps an old lady can be mugged by some young thug in a police procedural soap opera. Perhaps one character in a family saga can be a loveable old granddad who is steadily losing his marbles. But old people are rare on our television screens. The old are not perceived to be interesting. In real life, all sorts of dramas beset old people. There is retirement, chronic illness, infirmity and dementia, to name but the most common, but such conditions are scarcely mentioned in the mass media. The general public does not want to know about them.

The physical changes associated with aging

As people grow older, they experience a decline in hormonal substances (such as oestrogen and testosterone); this results in the classic signs of aging including less smooth skin, less hair, less hair colour, and a reduction in height. In addition, the aging process affects hearing, vision, touch, smell and taste. There is also a decline in the effectiveness of the immune system. As a result, individuals become more susceptible to influenza, pneumonia and other infections. Even though moderate exercise and a healthy diet can help to delay the effects of aging, physical deterioration is inevitable. By the time the age of eighty is reached, the lungs have lost nearly half their capacity. At the same time, the whole muscular-skeletal system loses its strength, causing stiff joints and weak muscles. The slowing down of the body's systems also affects digestion. Further, the capacity of the brain to process information is also diminished as brain cells are lost and not replaced.

Jane H. had been a very beautiful girl. Her red-gold hair, delicate features and slender figure had been much admired and, as a teenager, she had always been surrounded by a crowd of adoring admirers. She married the son of a very rich man, ten years older than herself, at the age of nineteen. She was happy to settle down into a life of comfortable affluence. Over the course of time, two children appeared, a boy and then a girl. Both were lovely children and it seemed as if Jane had everything life could offer.

Sadly, things do not always run smoothly. Her husband was not quite as successful at making money as his father had been. Her son lacked drive and ambition; he was inclined to put on weight and without actually coming out as a homosexual, he showed no interest in girls. The daughter was very wild. She married for the first time at the age of seventeen, before she had even finished high school. She had three children in quick succession, but showed no aptitude for motherhood. By the time she was twenty-five, she was divorced; the courts had deemed that she was an unfit parent and the estranged husband was awarded custody. Subsequently she went on to marry four other men, each more unsatisfactory than the last.

These troubles took their toll on Jane's looks. Although she had always followed a strict beauty regime and a stringent programme of diet and exercise, by the time she was forty-five her figure had become a little less firm, she was colouring her hair every three weeks and her facial features had begun to sag. But Jane was committed to her appearance. Her beauty was an essential part of herself. Her visits to the hairdresser, beautician and gym became more and more frequent.

Then she embarked on plastic surgery. First it was a small eye-lift to widen her eyes to give them a more child-like gaze. She was so pleased with the result, that she decided on a full first face-lift. There was no doubt that the result was excellent. Friends told her that she looked as good as ever. Her confidence returned and she became her old arch, flirtatious self again. Nonetheless as the months and years passed, there could be no relaxation. Again and again she had to return to the surgeon to have small surgical adjustments. By the time she was fifty-five, she was ready for her second face-lift and she had a third one in her early sixties. Her facial expressions were becoming fixed and tight and each operation was less successful than the one before.

She had always been aware that less could be done for her body. She continued to follow her punishing regime of diet and exercise and, as the years passed, she wore slightly more concealing clothes. The real blow occurred when she started to suffer from severe arthritis in her mid-sixties. The doctors told her that over-exercising was one of the causes of the problem. She had two hip replacements, but nothing could be done for the arthritis in her spine. Also one of her knees was constantly painful. Before long a stair-lift had to be installed in her house. By the time she was seventy, she was still, at first sight, a beautiful woman with the same extraordinary red-gold hair. But she was very lame. She needed to walk with a stick and all too often she retreated to a wheel chair, pushed by her long-suffering husband. After all, she was no longer a young woman.

As she grew more infirm, she became more and more unhappy. She had never had any real interests beyond herself, her family and her appearance. In the past that had been enough. Now her children were less than attentive. They made no secret of the fact that they blamed her narcissism for many of their problems. Her husband had health difficulties of his own. He was nearing eighty by this time. There were no longer hoards of admirers crowding round. She had become an old lady, crippled, without resources and of little interest to anyone. She could easily live another twenty years, but there was not much to look forward to.

Vision

An important characteristic of aging is that the lens of the eye begins to become more rigid. This leads to long-sightedness (known as presbyopia) whereby the eye cannot focus on close objects. This condition is typically first noticed before the age of fifty and, by the age of sixty or seventy, it is likely to be very pronounced. Glare from oncoming headlights also becomes a problem for night-time driving. In dimly lit rooms, the elderly find it difficult to see, and refocusing takes longer when going from light to dark rooms. Further, it becomes harder to distinguish between colours, and contrasts and shadows become more difficult to interpret, making it more perilous to go down steps.

Almost everyone suffers from presbyopia as they grow older, but there are also four major eye diseases which commonly affect older people:

(1) Cataracts

Having cataracts is like looking through glasses smeared with Vaseline. This is because the transparent lens of the eye become filmy. All the light entering the eye passes through the lens and if any part of the lens distorts or diffuses incoming light, vision is impaired. Cataracts can also block bright light from being diffused: this trapped light produces halos around lights, scattered light and glare. By the age of sixty-five, it is common to have mild cataracts. If they become severe and disturb vision, cataract surgery is required to replace the lens. This is generally very successful, but can lead to complications.

(2) Glaucoma

Glaucoma can result in partial or total blindness. It is caused by pressure on the eye which increases to such a degree that it damages the optic nerve. Such pressure is caused by fluid inside the eye that fails to drain; this results in a loss in peripheral vision. Treatment for this disease ranges from medication to laser therapy and surgery. Again the treatment, if done early enough, can be very successful, but it is important to have eyes tested regularly so that the condition is detected as soon as it appears.

(3) Macular degeneration

The macula is the central area of the retina which focuses on details in the centre of the field of vision. When the macula begins degenerating, straight lines are seen as wavy; blind spots appear in the centre of vision. Dry macular degeneration occurs when a pigment is deposited in the macula with no scarring, blood or fluid leakage; wet degeneration takes place when there is leakage including small haemorrhages surrounding the macula. There is little treatment for this condition, although when new blood vessels grow around the macula, laser surgery can be used to remove them. Macular degeneration rarely causes total blindness, but it can result in an almost complete loss of central vision. For a person in the advanced stages of the disease, reading becomes impossible and recognising people from their appearance becomes increasingly difficult.

(4) Diabetic retinopathy

Diabetes, an increasingly common disease in our affluent society, can also affect the eyes. High blood sugar levels make the walls of the small blood vessels in the retina thicker and weaker; this produces leaks and deformity and results in blurred vision and blindness. The best remedy is prevention by controlling glucose levels and blood pressure. However this does require real discipline in the matter of diet and many elderly people who are used to a diet high in fats and sugar find this difficult.

Julian J. was diagnosed as a diabetic in his early fifties. He worked as a travelling salesman and he ate many of his meals in hotels as he travelled about the country for his bespoke clothing firm. He had always loved his food and he enjoyed trying new dishes; his wife was an excellent cook and he had been brought up in a household in which everyone was encouraged to eat every crumb and then to have a second helping. The diagnosis of diabetes was a tremendous jolt. Initially Julian had every intention of sticking to the diet which the doctor had given him. Very soon however he was beginning to cheat. His problem was he just could not resist rich things, particularly sweet, creamy desserts. Soon he was back to his old ways. By the time he was sixty, his sight was largely gone and he was registered as blind. He had had to retire at the early age of fifty-seven because he could no longer drive his car and he was, in effect, confined to the house. Under his wife's supervision, he was forced to stick to his diet and gradually his condition stabilized. It seemed there was every likelihood he would live many more years. However he was going to spend the rest of his life as a blind man. Fiercely independent throughout his professional career, he now had to rely on others for all the necessities of life. His entertainment was to be largely confined to the radio and to talking books and his only direct contact with the outside world was when old friends were kind enough to drop in to see him. It was a gloomy prospect for the next few decades.

Hearing

Deafness is often a major problem for the elderly. By the age of sixty, one out of three people experience hearing loss. The majority of those over seventy-five have difficulties hearing. Carrying on a conversation with someone who cannot hear well is exhausting. Social interaction becomes more limited. The deaf become irritable because they misunderstand what is said to them, and they often withdraw from conversation. Inevitably the speaker is compelled to shout, and this is all too easily interpreted as insulting behaviour. In addition the old often resist purchasing or wearing a hearing aid. It is seen as a major defeat in the battle against old age, and in any case, many people find them difficult to use. The batteries are small and fiddly to put in for old, arthritic hands. The aid itself is often hard to insert in the ear and is seen to be intrusive. Background noise becomes a problem since the aid magnifies everything, not just the conversation the wearer wants to hear. Sufferers need to be reassured that today's models are almost invisible. Many are even computerized and can adjust the background noise level to some extent. Beyond this, there are a number of practical steps that can be taken to overcome misunderstanding in conversation:

- Talk more slowly
- Pronounce words carefully
- Indicate at the start of the conversation what is to be discussed
- Use facial expressions and gestures to convey meaning
- Make sure you are both looking at one another
- Eliminate background noise

Diabetes

Nearly one in twelve people over the age of sixty-five is afflicted with Type 2 diabetes; of those over the age of eighty-five, the figure is one in four. It is the seventh most common cause of death among the elderly, and the main cause of blindness. If old people begin to complain of fatigue, weight loss, blurred vision, hunger, thirst or itchy skin, they should see a doctor. In all likelihood a change in life-style will be recommended. This will include losing weight, exercising regularly and changing diet. Insulin therapy might also be suggested. As time goes on, it may become necessary to prepare special diabetic-friendly meals and freeze them for future use. It is very important that the old person sticks to his or her diet (see the case of Julian J. above) and a certain amount of supervision will probably be necessary.

Osteoporosis

One in four women is likely to suffer broken bones from osteoporosis by the time they reach eighty-five; a third will have broken a hip by the age of ninety. The term osteoporosis means porous bones. Those most at risk are Caucasians, those who are thin and small-boned, those who smoke and drink alcohol excessively, and those who experienced an early menopause. There is good evidence to show that hormone replacement therapy after the menopause does much to protect against the disease, but, unfortunately, it does have other less desirable side-effects. In any event, all post-menopausal women should eat a calcium-rich diet and possibly take calcium tablets as well as additional Vitamin D. This helps the bones to absorb calcium. It is also important to take exercise. An obvious precaution for the elderly is to wear sturdy shoes to prevent falls and to install hand rails around the house.

By the time Margaret H. reached her eighties, she was aware that many of her friends had had nasty falls, had broken bones and that it had taken some time for the bones to knit again. She used to quote these old ladies saying, 'I've never been the same since my fall...' Sadly, her time was coming. She had always been a highly involved and active person and one day she took a bus to visit a friend in the north of the city. No one knew quite what happened. She probably missed her footing as she got out at her bus stop, but it ended with her being taken in an ambulance to hospital. There she was diagnosed as having a broken hip and quite severe osteoporosis. The doctor told her she was lucky that it had not happened before. Through determination and careful physiotherapy, she did become mobile again, but it was a real struggle. She was never again the confident, independent person she had been.

Of course accidents such as falling off a bus can happen to anyone, but there is no doubt that Margaret would have been less vulnerable if she had taken extra calcium regularly through her fifties, sixties and seventies.

Arthritis

Arthritis means inflammation and refers to a disease of the joints. Typically joints become red, swollen, stiff and painful. There are two major reasons for this: firstly, the cartilage between connecting bones wears thin, and, secondly, joint tissues are destroyed by changes in their biochemical composition. The most common arthritic conditions are:

1. Osteoarthritis
Here cartilage in the joints has become thin and frayed. This causes the joints to swell. Usually hands, feet, hips, knees and back are affected.

2. Rheumatoid arthritis

This affects the entire body. The immune system attacks the joints as well as connective tissues in the tendons of the joints, heart and lungs. Symptoms include soreness, stiffness, aching joints and fatigue.

Both these types of arthritis are normally treated with pain killers. In more serious cases, surgical procedures such as hip and knee replacements can be very effective.

3. Gout

This is typically a male complaint, although women can get it too. Uric acid builds up and forms crystals in the joints. They affect the big toe, foot, ankle, knee and wrist. It is important for those afflicted to consume foods with a high purine content such as beer. In addition there are drugs which can lessen pain during an attack.

Chronic obstructive pulmonary disease

This is a lung disease referring to emphysema and chronic bronchitis. Men are more likely than women to suffer from these and the main cause is smoking. In cases of emphysema, lung tissue breaks down and is replaced by empty space. Stale air gets trapped and prevents oxygen from being exchanged. In bronchitis the bronchi produce excessive mucus which has to be shifted by constant coughing. There are numerous treatments for these respiratory conditions, the most important of which is to stop smoking immediately. In serious cases sufferers should be seen by a lung specialist and oxygen may be prescribed.

Sleep disorder

It is common for the elderly to have difficulty with sleep. This is because there are fewer brain cells and less of the melatonin hormone, both of which regulate deep sleep. Old people all too often take too little exercise, drink too much coffee and tea and continue to smoke. All these factors contribute to restlessness at night.

There are a number of ways that the problem can be combated:

- Follow a soothing pattern for going to bed, including listening to music or reading
- Go to bed at the same time each night
- Take regular exercise
- Limit coffee and tea intake
- Limit naps to the afternoon
- Avoid eating large meals before bedtime
- Refrain from smoking
- Avoid alcohol before bed

It is important not to depend on sleeping pills which can become addictive. Instead the elderly should be encouraged to follow a sensible and regular sleep routine.

Mabel S was a sensitive, highly-strung woman. She had never been a good sleeper. She liked to stay up late chatting, drinking coffee and listening to music. She was devoted to late-night television. As a young woman she had found it very difficult to get up in the morning, but she came alive during the hours of darkness. By the time she reached her late seventies and eighties, she was finding sleep more and more difficult. Night after night she would lie awake listening to her grandfather clock striking the hours. Eventually she went to the doctor and demanded sleeping pills. The doctor had a lot of people waiting in his surgery. Instead of discussing natural methods to induce sleep, he gave her what she asked, but with stern injunctions not to take more than one a night.

To begin with everything was fine. With the aid of the pills, Mabel found it far easier to get to sleep. But over the years her body became used to them. They ceased to be so effective and she was tempted to take a second one if she woke in the early hours. She lived alone and no one was really monitoring the situation.

The surgery would give her more pills whenever she asked for a repeat prescription. Then, in her late eighties, she started to get confused. Increasingly she was forgetting people's names and was repeating herself on the telephone. Some days she seemed much more bewildered than others. It became clear that she no longer really remembered whether she had taken her sleeping pill or not. By this stage she was dependant on them and cutting them out completely was not an option. Yet who knew how many she was really taking? Her children began to have serious fears of an accidental overdose...

Temperature change

As people grow older, their brain's ability to determine temperature changes lessens and this is complicated by circulatory problems and medications. Even the body's ability to sweat is affected. To combat these difficulties in hot weather, the old should be encouraged to drink fluids, use fans and air conditioning and apply a cool, wet cloth to the back of the head if necessary. If it is cold, they should turn up the heating and cover themselves with warm blankets.

Incontinence

To a greater or lesser extent, this affects millions of old people and it is most common among women. Medications, dementia and urinary tract infections as well as endocrine problems can cause the problem. There are three types of incontinence:

1. Stress incontinence. This occurs when the muscles of the pelvic floor become weakened due to childbirth or hormonal change. The bladder then slips down without muscle support and abdominal muscles squeeze the bladder.
2. Overflow incontinence. Here urine in the bladder reaches

a point where the muscle which controls the flow is unable to function properly. Urine then leaks out.

3. Urge incontinence. In this case an individual will feel an urgent need to urinate. There is little time between feeling the need and actually urinating. In cases where there has been a stroke or there is significant dementia, the brain is, in any case, unable to send appropriate signals and the patient becomes incontinent.

Various measures can be taken to deal with the problem:

- Organize a regular schedule to go to the bathroom
- Ensure that the path to the bathroom is clear
- If possible, a second bathroom should be installed
- Eliminate drinks before going to bed
- Avoid foods that contain sugar, chocolate, and hot spices
- When going out, be aware of the location of the nearest toilet
- Avoid smoking

In serious cases, medications can be used to help relax the bladder muscles. For women, it is also possible to use a urethral plug or a foam pad. In some cases surgery can remove a blockage, repair the urethra, or reposition the bladder; as a final resort catheters can be placed into the bladder through the urethra. It may be that the best option is to wear incontinence pads. If so, it is important that they are changed very frequently to avoid skin infections and irritation. Although it is much feared by the elderly themselves and by their families, incontinence is very common among old people and it can be managed very effectively.

Strokes

The effect of a stroke is to stop the blood supply to the brain. An artery may be clogged or a vessel tears, leaking the blood before and after it reaches the brain. This can result in serious damage to brain cells. There are a number of types of strokes, some more serious than others:

1. Transient ischemic attacks. Here the attack occurs suddenly and usually lasts from two to thirty minutes. There is thus a short-term deficiency in the brain's blood supply. The symptoms are similar to a stroke but they are temporary. The patient may become dizzy, be unable to see, or slur speech. If any such episode occurs, a doctor should be consulted as soon as possible.
2. Ischemic stroke. In such cases an artery carrying blood to the brain is blocked. This can result in permanent damage to the brain.
3. Hemorrhagic stroke. In this case the vessel carrying blood and oxygen bursts and leaks blood into the brain. Brain cells are thereby destroyed. The following are signals of such strokes:
- Weakness or numbness of the face, arm and leg on one side of the body
- Confusion, trouble speaking or understanding
- Dimness or loss of vision
- Trouble walking, dizziness, loss of balance
- Severe headache

If someone has a stroke, the first two days are vital for making a good recovery. The doctor might order a CT scan or an MRI. Rehabilitation takes time and the patient will need a great deal of support. It is possible to prevent strokes by attending to:

1. **High blood pressure.** Here it is important to have a well balanced diet, attain a suitable weight, and take exercise. Medication can also be very effective in controlling the condition.
2. **Cigarette smoking.** By eliminating smoking, the risk of a stroke is substantially reduced.
3. **Diabetes.** Diabetes should be controlled to avoid any complications.

4. Heart Disease. A regular dosage of aspirin can help prevent clotting.

Heart attacks

Like strokes, heart attacks can afflict people of any age, but the elderly are particularly susceptible. Four out of five of those who have heart attacks are over sixty-five. Those most at risk include: smokers, the overweight, those with high blood pressure, those with high cholesterol, those suffering from diabetes, and individuals who are under stress. There are a number of ways of preventing heart attacks.

- People with high blood pressure should be careful about their diet, reduce salt intake, control weight, manage stress, and take medication for the condition
- Those with high cholesterol should follow a low cholesterol diet
- Persons who suffer from angina can be treated by the doctor. If he discovers that an artery or vein is blocked, a tiny balloon can be inserted to open up the vessel, and then a stent can be inserted to keep the vessel open or bypass the blocked vessel. Medication can also help
- If there is congestive heart failure, the doctor will also prescribe medication

The most common symptoms of a heart attack are:

- Feelings of pressure, fullness, or pain in the centre of the chest
- Pain spreading from the shoulders, neck or arm
- Chest, stomach or abdominal pain
- Nausea or dizziness
- Shortness of breath and difficulty breathing
- Anxiety, weakness or fatigue
- Palpitations, cold sweat, and excessive pallor

Cancer

Cancer occurs when cancer cells multiply and produce a tumour. The disease can attack many different parts of the body and, if unchecked, can move from one organ to another through the blood system. The initial symptoms are:

- A sore that does not heal
- Changes in a mole or wart
- Blood in the urine
- Persistent constipation or a change in bowel movements
- Constant stomach pain
- Sore throat or difficulty swallowing
- Cough, hoarseness, difficulty breathing
- Constant pain in any part of the body
- Lump in the breast, vulva, neck, head or other part of the body

If any of these symptoms occur, a doctor should be seen as a matter of urgency. In the majority of cases the symptoms will not turn out not to be caused by cancer. Many cancers are, in any case, completely curable and prognosis and treatments are improving all the time. To avoid the disease, a healthy diet should be eaten, smoking should be avoided and it is sensible to have regular medical check-ups.

As a result of a routine medical check, Susan P. was diagnosed with breast cancer in her late sixties. She was surprised. There was no history of cancer in her family and, from all the scare stories in the newspapers, she had the vague idea that breast cancer was a danger to young women. Her doctor told her that in fact breast cancer was much more common in older women. She followed the doctor's advice meticulously. A surgeon removed the lump and she went through a course of radiotherapy. She took all the medications prescribed and she was conscientious in attending her regular check-ups. Although she was warned that a recurrence was possible, she had no more trouble. In the end she died of a stroke at the age of ninety-four.

Dementia

The term dementia refers to the loss of cerebral ability. The leading cause of dementia is Alzheimer's, a progressive brain disease. It can also be caused by a series of mini-strokes which cause the death of brain cells. These small successive strokes are often unobserved – those with high blood pressure and diabetes are particularly susceptible. There are, however, a number of warning signs of the onset of Alzheimer's.

1. Memory loss affecting skills at work
2. Difficulty performing familiar tasks
3. Problems with language
4. Disorientation to time and place
5. Lack of judgment
6. Problems with abstract thought
7. Misplacing objects
8. Mood and behavioural change
9. Change in personality
7. Loss of initiative

There are three main stages of Alzheimer's:

- **Stage 1.** There is still an ability to remember recent events. Speech may be impaired, and there is difficulty remembering the correct word. The sufferer may be careless about grooming, and become irritable
- **Stage 2.** Behaviour becomes more extreme. Short term memory disappears and help will be needed in dressing, eating and bathing. The patient may become easily agitated and wander or pace back and forth. Sleep cycles can also become disturbed.
- **Stage 3.** Here long term memory will have also faded, and the person will need total care. There may also be a degree of paranoia. Joints become rigid, and the range of motion will be

limited. Eventually the patient will become bedridden, unable to speak, communicate or feed herself. The immune system can also be seriously affected, providing opportunities for infection.

It must be stressed that some form of dementia is extremely common in old people. It has been calculated that among ninety-year olds, one person in four is a sufferer. As people live longer, inevitably dementia in one form or other will become an increasing problem in society.

Her friends began to notice that Jean A. was becoming more forgetful by the time she was in her early eighties. To begin with it was funny. She and her husband had decided it was time to move into sheltered accommodation and she was dismantling the house she had lived in for thirty years. Many things had to be disposed of and Jean kept making a present of the same object to more than one friend. Once she had moved into the new apartment, her mental state grew rapidly worse. It took her a long time to settle in her new surroundings and she was noticeably more confused. Her husband also found the change difficult. He was not happy and within six months he had had a major stroke and had to be moved to a nursing home.

Jean was increasingly looked after by aides who came in at certain times every day to get her up in the morning, to give her a shower, to prepare her meals and to help her into bed. As the months passed, her short-term memory faded. She had no idea what she had done the day before. When friends and family visited, she had no recollection of their visits. Over time, she ceased to recognize people, but, despite this, for several years she could still recall incidents from her childhood and would talk about people who were long since dead. She became incontinent and started wandering about the building. By this stage she needed constant supervision and she had to be moved to a secure nursing home.

By the time she died in her mid-nineties, she could no longer remember her own name. All traces of identity had been lost.

The above catalogue gives a gloomy picture of extreme old age. Yet it does not have to be an unhappy time. The ideal is to avoid these ills and remain healthy and to enjoy life for as long as possible. This is what we all want for our parents and it is the aim of this book, if at all possible, to help the reader achieve it.

2

Caring for parents

BOOKS DEALING WITH elderly care often refer to parents as Mom and Dad. They take it for granted that children will be determined to do their best for their parents at all costs. The presupposition is that children owe this to their mother and father, presumably because of the parents' devoted care throughout childhood and young adulthood. The appeal is always to emotion, sentimentality and familial loyalty. Although there is some acknowledgement of the physical and financial problems of caring for the aging, all too often the serious emotional difficulties faced by both children and parents are blithely ignored. In short, readers of such books are given only a partial perception of all the complications involved.

There is no question that Sylvia L. had neglected her daughters when they were young. She had had a moderately successful career as a character actress; she had married one of her directors and had been determined to continue her career as long as possible. She had always loved parties, showing off and basking in male admiration. She had never really wanted to have children, but, at the very least, she expected them to be boys. When the second daughter appeared, she gave up all pretence of domesticity and handed over the girls first to a series of unsatisfactory mother's helps and then, as soon as they were old enough, to boarding schools. She was not a bad woman, but she had nothing in common with her daughters. They had not inherited her good looks and, as they grew up, instead of being lively and a magnet for boys (Sylvia would have enjoyed a constant stream of young men through the house) they were both studious and shy. In the course of time they both did get married, but Sylvia found her sons-in-law equally disappointing. One worked in a high street bank and the other was a lawyer in a country town.

Sylvia became a widow in her mid-seventies. She did not like it, but after a short and fruitless search for another husband, she realized it was a hopeless quest and she settled down into complaining invalidism. At this point she wanted her daughters. She could not understand why both girls did not drop everything and come to look after her. She telephoned them both every day to tell them at length about her ailments; in a performance which did credit to her dramatic past she would declare her undying love for them. She would describe her acute loneliness and would insist that it could only be alleviated if they came to live with her. When they suggested that she go into an old peoples' home where she would be looked after and have companionship, she would scream in protest. "But that's what family's for!"

The need for realism

What should be the basis for care of the elderly? It is generally taken for granted that children should be responsible for their parents because they love them. Religious principles are invoked such as the Biblical commandment: 'Honour your father and your mother' (Exodus 20:12). The following, from a Jewish guide to elderly care, is a typical example of such advice:

Because of God's involvement in everything the child should be grateful for – life, nurturing, and so forth – ingratitude to parents is seen as leading to or even as an actual expression of ingratitude to God and a denigration or denial of God's historical and covenantal relationship with Israel. Children do not merely repay their parents for services rendered to them in their childhood; rather, they act on the basis of an interpersonal relationship that is a microcosm of their relationship with God.

The assumption here is that children should act out of gratitude, and that just as parents have been responsible for their children in the past, so children should be responsible for their parents when they are old. However, what such care manuals overlook is that in many cases family life has been fraught with difficulties. Parents and children do not always get along. Sibling rivalry is often intense. Further, the costs of medical care, residential accommodation and nursing homes can be catastrophic for a family's finances; in many cases they will exhaust the estate of elderly parents. Such a prospect may cause ambivalence at the very least amongst children.

In light of such dilemmas, it is vital that children are honest with themselves about how they plan to deal with their parents' aging. In many instances, they may want to be of assistance because of genuine affection. In other cases, care for the elderly may be based only on a sense of duty. It is arguable that the latter motive may prove the more reliable given the complexities of the problems connected with aging. It may be far more helpful to set aside one's feelings and focus instead on concrete, measurable objectives such as organizing home nursing care or finding a suitable nursing home. While parents want love from their children, what they need most is practical help in an environment in which they can cope adequately.

The following is a checklist to test real feelings about parents:

- Do you think your mother and father were good, caring parents?

- Did you suffer physical, sexual or emotional abuse from either parent?
- Have you experienced serious conflict with either your mother or your father?
- Were your parents financially generous to you?
- Did your parents neglect you during your early childhood, adolescence or early adulthood?
- Do you genuinely feel responsibility towards your parents?
- To what degree are you prepared to look after them?
- Would you have your parents live at home with you?
- Are you prepared to pay for your parents' medical expenses if this proves necessary?
- Are you willing to visit your parents if they are in a nursing home?
- What does your spouse feel about the situation?

Medical costs

In both the US and Britain, private medical costs can be astronomic. While both countries do provide a public health service, it is not for those who have even a modest estate. People who have worked hard all their lives and have prudently put money away are treated in the same way as the very rich. They are compelled to pay for their own care until the estate is more or less exhausted. In the UK (but not in the US) doctors and medicines are paid for by the National Health Service, but the cost of a private nursing home in both countries can be well over £1000 ($1800) per week.

For the elderly struggling to cope with the onset of physical disabilities, the thought of such expenditure can be deeply alarming. Their children may be equally agitated by the prospect. In some cases, children may even have relied on their parents' money to pay for their own children's college fees or merely to support their desired lifestyle. Such a situation is a recipe for resentment on the one side and guilt on the other.

Harry T. had always been careful with money. He had worked all his life as a middle manager in a confectionary firm. He and his wife bought their own modest home, brought up their children frugally and had a comfortable 'nest-egg' in the bank. Although his wife died of cancer in her late sixties, Harry remained ferociously independent, paying his own way and owing nothing to anyone.

His brother Gerald was a very different character. He had gone through a host of different jobs during his working life, always expecting to earn a fortune around the next corner. Over the years he also managed to discard no fewer than three wives. When he reached the age to retire, he was in a poor state. He had been compelled to give the (heavily mortgaged) family home to his last wife and he largely lived on state handouts and the occasional present from Harry or his children.

When they were in their early eighties, both brothers were diagnosed with Parkinson's Disease. They both needed residential care and they ended up in the same nursing home. Harry had to pay the entire cost of his care himself. Gerald, being more or less indigent, had his fees paid for him by the State. It is not surprising that when Harry's middle-aged children visited their father and uncle and saw any money they might have inherited being used to pay for something their uncle got for nothing, life did not seem fair.

Wills

Parents should have made their wills many years before they reach old age. It should be stressed, however, that not every written document that sets out how property is to be disposed of on death is a will. It must be signed properly in the presence of witnesses who are not beneficiaries. The testator must be of sound mind and cannot have been put under physical or emotional pressure. However wills should be regularly updated as familial circumstances change. Great care must be taken when encouraging an elderly member of a family to make or change a will to ensure that it does not merely set out the wishes of the person doing the encouraging! If the testator is unduly persuaded or is of unsound mind, the probate courts may rule that the will is invalid. When a very aged person makes a will, it is a sensible idea that the testator's doctor act as one of the witnesses. He or she should check that the person is not only capable of making a will, but that its contents are understood.

There are rules about how to sign and witness a will:

- the will must be in writing
- it must be signed by the person making the will
- the signature must be witnessed by at least two independent witnesses
- The witnesses may not be left anything in the will

A will that conforms to these rules will be upheld by the courts, and its instructions must be followed . This is so even if the person making the will has made a mistake. Only if there is some ambiguity will the court consider other evidence. If the will does turn out to be ambiguous, there are serious consequences. The gift might not go to the correct person. For example, if a man leaves his property to 'my children' and at death he has four children including one stepchild, the law will construe 'my children' as meaning only his own children. The claims of the step-child will be ignored. The gift might even fail altogether because the court cannot decide the will's meaning. To avoid such difficulties, a will should use clear and unambiguous language and preferably be drawn up by a lawyer. Anyone who doubts the importance of a clearly-worded will should read *Bleak House* by Charles Dickens, a cautionary tale of what can happen if a will is ambiguous.

Some of the words used in wills include:

- bequeath – this refers to a gift of anything other than land. 'Land' includes houses, apartments and open spaces. If the gift is of land, the word 'devise' should be used.
- children – this includes both legitimate and illegitimate

children, both boys and girls. Adopted children are included
if the will was made before or after the date of the formal
adoption order. Stepchildren do not necessarily come
within the definition of 'children' unless all the children are
stepchildren and there are no other children alive at the date
of the will.

- descendents – this refers to children, grandchildren, great-
grandchildren, great-great grandchildren, both male and
female. If the property is left to 'all my descendents', each
descendent will have an equal share of the estate.
- family – this term has been held to have several meanings.
Generally it means the same as 'children', but there may be
some confusion if the term is used. 'A child of the family' is
one treated as one of the family whoever their parents. This
can be different from 'a child of the marriage.'
- infant – this refers to a minor, a person under 18
- issue – this means the same as 'descendants'
- legacy – this refers to a specific sum left to a beneficiary
- nephews and nieces – this includes only the nephews and
nieces of the person who writes the will, not the nephews and
nieces of his or her spouse
- next of kin – this is the person who is the closest blood
relative of the person writing the will
- residue – this is what is left after paying expenses, inheritance
tax, and legacies

It is important to plan ahead and envisage all circumstances that
might apply when a will is written. Inevitably, the distribution of
an estate can lead to severe conflict among children and any other
beneficiaries. It is vital that the intentions of the person making the
will are clear, and that it is understood who should receive money
and possessions. Because of the potential difficulties connected with
an estate, it is preferable if the person who makes a will discusses his
or her intentions with their children. Ideally they should see the will
in advance so there is no uncertainty.

Frances T. had always enjoyed manipulating people. She had been left a large sum of money by her husband who had been an eminent scientist and inventor. He had been a widower when he married her and there was a son of the previous marriage. She herself had had two daughters. She was on reasonable terms with all three children, who by the time she was in her eighties were in their fifties and sixties. However, she had always been secretive as to how she was going to leave the money. She had certainly given her step-son to understand that he would be included (after all it was originally his father's money) and that the money would be divided according to the children's attentiveness towards her.

In the event, although over the years Frances had made several wills with a lawyer, the final will was handwritten. It was signed in the nursing home and had been witnessed by two of the cleaners. Composed of one sentence it read, 'I leave everything to my children.'

This meant that the step-son was not included. He was sure that this had not been his step-mother's intention and he asked his sisters if they were willing to allocate him a reasonable share. The younger sister was resentful. She was not well-off and she had done a great deal for her mother. The elder girl was married to a millionaire and had visited only occasionally. No one was prepared to compromise. In the end it went through the courts. The cost of lawyers was enormous and it ended with the whole estate being substantially diminished. This is not what Frances would have wanted.

Intestacy

If there is no will, property must be disposed of according to a set legal formula which includes all members of the immediate family. This is highly unlikely to be in accordance with the wishes of the elderly person. Thus it is very important that future mortality is confronted and a will is made.

Sibling rivalry

Conflict between children is common and can lead to bitter family arguments when parents become elderly. Who is to make decisions about the welfare of a mother or father? Should responsibilities be shared equally? Is it the duty of both sons and daughters to share in the physical burden of care? Who is to have power of attorney? Should any of the children serve as guardians or conservators? Is a parent to live at home with one of the children? Who should act as executors of the will? Should any child have a greater share of the inheritance? Should all children have equal responsibilities for visiting and looking after parents? Who is to make the decision about whether a parent should move into an old people's home or a nursing home? Should such decisions be shared by all children? What happens if they disagree? Inevitably, the history of family conflict in the past will influence the answers to these questions. All too often, the problems of aging parents can open old wounds.

Marcia G. and her husband Frank had two daughters. The elder was beautiful. She had blonde curly hair, delicate features and and a way with her. Frank adored her. He was involved in the fashion business and he loved bringing home samples from the latest designers for her to wear. He insisted that she went to the best hairdresser in town and although the family was not rich, he even bought her a beautiful leopard skin jacket (this was in the 1950s before such jackets were banned). She looked like a young movie star.

By contrast the younger girl was plain and podgy. Her hair was ginger. She had had a long period of sickness as a child and she remained pasty and hypochondriacal. Her father had little time for her. In fact she was a clever girl who did well at school, but this was of little interest to Frank. He found her dull and tiresome; he resented paying college fees and he made no secret of the fact that he thought she should find herself a husband as quickly as possible.

Time passed and, on her twentieth birthday, the elder girl

married. It was all highly satisfactory. The young man was not only extremely good-looking; he was also the only son of a very prosperous businessman. There was a thriving real-estate business to take over. Sadly it was at the other end of the country and, in the future, only one visit a year could be hoped for, but it was a brilliant match and Frank and Marcia were thrilled. Later the younger girl also married. She found a doctor ten years older than herself. There was no family money and he was not an easy person, but he was a clever man and had good prospects. The couple bought a house close to Frank and Marcia.

After Marcia became a widow, she was looked after entirely by the younger daughter. The marriage had not been particularly happy. There was no divorce, but her mother's house was a retreat. Once she had become middle-aged and her only child was in college, she was happy to spend much of her time looking after her mother. In fact she did not even welcome her sister's annual visit. The two had never got on and, even after Frank's death, the sibling rivalry remained.

The businessman son-in-law had tried to persuade Marcia to leave her money equally between the grandchildren. He argued that it would save inheritance tax. The younger daughter was furious. Her sister had two children while she only had one. The doctor's son-in-law made it clear that he felt his wife should have the lion's share; after all she was the one who was bearing the burden of Marcia's care. In the event, Marcia left it equally between her two daughters, but there was still an ugly scene after the funeral. The younger sister was going to have to do all the clearing up since her sister was returning home as soon as possible. This did not stop the elder sister marching into the apartment and demanding all the family's sentimental treasures. "After all," she said, "I'm the eldest and I was Dad's favourite."

Parental support

In some cases, parents will have the financial resources for their own care. In other instances, they will not have been able to save enough money. Who then is to provide support? This burden traditionally has fallen upon children, but such responsibility can lead to hardship and conflict. Do children have the duty to pay for medical care and nursing home accommodation for their aging parents? The answer to this question will depend on personal attitudes as well as the funds available. In some cases, children might feel that the welfare and education of their own children is a more important priority. One solution might be to have the parent live in one child's home. But, again, this could cause enormous disruption and dissension. If there are several children, it may be easier if only one child acts as the major support. But if this is agreed, is that child owed a greater proportion of a future inheritance? These issues are potentially fraught to put it mildly.

David G. was a university lecturer. His father had been an orthopaedic surgeon and had made a good living. David himself had grown up in a lovely house in one of the best suburbs and had been educated at Harvard. He confidently expected that his own son would follow in his footsteps. He was a clever boy. David knew that paying the fees would be a problem. The boy was not likely to be eligible for a scholarship; the family earned too much, but with fees of more than \$30,000 (£20,000) a year and two other children to take into account, it was more than a university salary could handle. However, David was not worried. His father was proud of the boy. By the time he was ready for college, the grandfather would be over eighty. David was an only child. He would either have inherited his father's money or his father would pay the fees.

It did not work out like that. David's father developed severe Alzheimer's disease in his late seventies. He was violent, recognized no-one and needed specialized nursing home care. This cost more than \$100,000 (£70,000) a year. David was appointed conservator of his father's money, but the court only allowed him to spend it on his father's care. There could be no provision for university fees and, in any case, the old man's money would not last forever. If he lived long enough, then David himself would have to find the nursing home fees. Certainly there could be no Harvard for the grandson. In the event, he had to go to the State University where the fees were much lower and he could live at home.

Nursing homes

Leaving home for residential care is traumatic. Old people may resist the transition even if there is a pressing need. How can such a decision be made? This is particularly difficult if a parent is determined to retain independence. Here there is a need for sensitivity as well as firmness. Children may feel guilty pressurizing their mother or father to make this change; parents may simply turn obstinate. Discussions with elderly parents who are hard of hearing, confused or fearful can often be frustrating, leaving all parties irritable and distraught. There are a number of issues that should be faced:

- Can the parent live on their own?
- Does the parent need assistance at home? If so, how much and for what?
- Is it feasible for a parent to live in a child's home? If so, who should bear such responsibility?
- Is it more suitable for a parent to live in a residential facility?
- What level of care is needed?
- Is there enough money to pay for either residential accommodation or a nursing home?
- Will the residence allow the parent to bring furniture?
- Are pets accepted in the residence?
- Is it important that children live near the residence?
- How often will children visit their parents if they live in a residential or nursing home?

Visiting parents

It is vital that the elderly do not feel forgotten and lonely. If they have to go into residential care, important decisions must be reached about visiting. Should there be a formal rota? Should all the children feel an equal responsibility? What if one child lives nearer than the others? Are daughters expected to do more than sons? If one child shoulders all the duties, should he or she derive special benefits when the estate is finally distributed? How should visiting be organized? How long should a visit last? What about taking the parent out of the residence for little excursions? Is this too unsettling? What about independent adventures? How long is it sensible for an older person to continue driving a car? These are serious and important questions which must be confronted.

Guardianship and conservatorship

If a parent can no longer manage his or her affairs because of physical or mental infirmity, it may be necessary to appoint a guardian and/or a conservator. It is common for children to take on this responsibility, but which child is the most appropriate? Should it be a son or a daughter? The eldest or the youngest? Laws concerning such a role vary from country to country. In Britain, guardians are appointed by the court and look after both the physical welfare and the financial affairs of the protected person . This is done by a deed of appointment. In the US, guardians have responsibility only for physical welfare; a conservator is appointed to deal with the financial side. Both positions are under the jurisdiction of the court. In some cases, although it is expensive, it might be preferable to hire professionals to take on these roles. But who is to make this decision? This is of considerable concern given the authority of guardians and conservators. If it is decided to avoid professional help, consideration needs to be given as to whether the child who undertakes such responsibility should also be remunerated.

Paula A. had two sons. Both were married, but one lived in the same town as she did while the other lived nearly five hundred miles away. Paula had been a careful, conscientious mother and both boys were fond of her, but, even as children, they had always disliked each other. When Paula showed the first signs of dementia and had to go into a home, it was clear that one of the boys needed to take charge of her affairs. It made sense that it should be the elder son who lived nearby. However, the two men did not trust each other and the younger son insisted that Paula be put under the guardianship of the court and that his brother be compelled to submit yearly accounts.

The younger boy perused these accounts carefully. A very great deal of money above and beyond the nursing home fees seemed to be spent on the old lady. However, when any item was questioned, the elder son always had a glib explanation. He also (as the court allowed him to do) paid himself for his duties as his mother's conservator. His younger brother thought his charges excessive, but they were passed without comment by the court.

When Paula died, she left her estate equally between her two sons. But the final years had proved very expensive. Very little was left. The younger son was convinced that his elder brother had been systematically helping himself from the estate and falsifying the accounts, but there was no way he could prove it. After the funeral, the brothers had no further contact.

Forgetfulness

Elderly parents who suffer from dementia may become particularly difficult to manage. This can lead to frustration and anger. Parents may become suspicious and irritable; children can become impatient. It is important for children to recognize that their parents are not being deliberately infuriating. They really have forgotten what they have been told or experienced. Tact and patience are essential. Once a form of dementia has been diagnosed, it is useful for children to read about the disease in its various forms.

Funerals

Arranging a funeral for a parent is also a potential area of conflict. Ideally a parent should have specified in his or her will what is preferred. This should minimize difficulties. Ideally, the children should know in advance whether the parent wishes to be cremated or buried and what, if any, religious service should take place. If there are no explicit instructions, things become more complicated. Children will need to decide what is best: Should the parent be buried or cremated? Should the funeral be religious or secular? If religious, according to which denomination? Should there be a memorial service later? What type of casket should be used? What kind of budget is envisaged? Who should pay if the parent has not made financial arrangements? These decisions have to be made swiftly, often while the family is still reeling from the shock of the death. It helps greatly if these matters have been discussed beforehand and agreed in outline.

Felicity M. had two children, a boy and a girl. The son was particularly close to his mother and had never married. The daughter lived about fifty miles away and was married to a Presbyterian minister. There were no instructions in the will and when Felicity died, the daughter felt the funeral service should take place in her husband's church and that he should lead the service. The son was appalled. Although she was not a churchgoer, his mother had been baptized an Anglican (Episcopalian). He insisted that the service should take place in the local Anglican church and that he should give the eulogy. He refused to allow his brother-in-law or sister any role in the arrangements. This quarrel poisoned the relationship between the two siblings and the funeral was a very awkward, unhappy occasion.

3

Managing health care

AGED PARENTS WILL inevitably need health care. As they get older, their bodies degenerate. They may have to cope with deafness, blindness, diabetes, arthritis, cancer, heart disease, incontinence and dementia. Faced with these problems, both parents and children will need to assess different courses of treatment. They will have to examine the different kinds of available care and the various accommodation possibilities. Ideally advice will be sought from professionals who specialize in geriatric ailments.

For several years Marion D. had suffered from macular degeneration. She was no longer able to read or drive, but this did not really matter. Her husband Tony looked after her. He had always been the main driver in the family and he had always dealt with the family's business documents. They had been married for over fifty-five years and, apart from Marion's blindness, they seemed in remarkably good health.

Sadly it was all to come to an end. Tony died very suddenly from a massive heart attack. Marion's children realized that something had to be done about their mother. They talked to her GP about the various alternatives. Before he gave any formal advice, he insisted that Marion should have a full medical examination. He discovered that she had quite severe osteoporosis; in fact it was surprising that she had not yet broken any bones. Even more seriously, she showed signs of confusion. After performing several cognitive tests, the doctor diagnosed the early stages of Alzheimer's disease.

It was clear that Marion was going to need a great deal of specialized help in the next few years. Her children had some hard decisions in front of them.

Organizing care

The first step in managing health care is to assemble all the necessary information. This should include:

- Insurance papers
- The names, addresses and telephone numbers of doctors, hospitals and health clinics
- A list of medications taken
- Copies of wills
- Background information on each diagnosed condition such as high blood pressure, diabetes, etc.
- A contact list including relatives, doctors, pharmacists, hospitals, health workers, social workers, etc.
- Copies of social security documents, Medicare and Medicaid in the US and National Insurance in the UK

With this information, the elderly person can be assessed by the doctor or a specialist geriatrician. After a full-scale examination, an analysis of the patient's condition will be produced. Various aspects will be evaluated, including range of motion, ability to walk, reach, bend, sustain balance, manage steps and the ease or difficulty in getting in and out of a chair. Possible dietary changes and needs will be also discussed and there will be an assessment of current cognitive functions, and mental health. Tests may include an electro-cardiograph, various blood tests, mental scans and a neurological evaluation. Once the tests are completed, the doctor will suggest a care plan which will meet the patient's needs. Only then should the family meet to discuss what should be done. If at all possible, the old person should be encouraged to participate in such a discussion. If distance makes such a conference impossible, absent family members can be included by telephone.

Long distance care

It is not uncommon for parents to live far away from their children and other family members. In such cases, it is important to make an accurate assessment of current living conditions. It may be necessary to rely on:

- Neighbours who can report on their welfare
- Post offices who, in the US, offer an elder-watch programme
- The bank, which can alert the family if something seems to be going wrong with financial management
- Local friends who see them regularly
- Community services which can offer both professional and voluntary help to the elderly
- Local minister, priest, imam or rabbi if they belong to a religious group

When making a visit to parents, it is important to be systematic in assessing their situation. It is helpful to have a checklist:

- Is mail being left unopened and are newspapers piling up?
- Are bills being paid on time?
- Is there an obvious change in activity level?
- Is there food in the refrigerator?

- Is the food in the refrigerator fresh and palatable?
- Is there an increasing tendency for parents to repeat themselves and do they seem to be more forgetful?
- Are tax returns and other documents being dealt with?
- Is the house reasonably clean?
- Does the elderly person seem to be clean?

If possible, it is useful to arrange to meet with the doctor and possibly even the dentist when on a visit. The children should be sure to leave contact details.

For many years Edward C. had lived with his English wife in the UK. He had grown up in California and his parents still lived there. As an only child, he was very conscious of the geographical distance between himself and his parents, but they were very rooted on the West Coast of America and his job and his wife's family were all in England. He made a point of telephoning every week and every year he and his wife went to stay in his parents' house. For many years the situation seemed stable. Edward's father was turning ninety and his mother was nearly eighty, but they seemed to be managing their lives successfully.

Then, two months before he was due for his annual visit, he received a telephone call from one of his parents' old friends. She too was over eighty, but Edward had known her all his life and he knew that she was unlikely to make a transatlantic telephone call without good reason. He was told that his parents were no longer eating properly. Mail lay around unopened. The house was untidy, even dirty; the elderly couple seemed depressed; they no longer socialized with their friends and were reluctant to leave the house. It was clear that they could no longer cope. Edward telephoned his parents' doctor and their parish priest, both of whom promised to go to the house. Three days later they both telephoned back and told very much the same story. Edward put forward his visit to California. He made arrangements to stay for a fortnight. He and his wife knew there was a great deal to be done and the upshot was that his parents were moved two months later into very attractive sheltered accommodation.

Care managers

In recent years, particularly in the US, there has been a growth in the number of professional care managers. These take on the task of organizing and coordinating the elderly person's care.

Typically care managers:

- conduct an assessment of the patient to identify the care required
- determine the eligibility of an older person for various services
- contact the relevant individuals and process the papers
- interview and monitor home care workers
- provide referrals to geriatric specialists and set up appointments for formal geriatric assessment
- arrange for transportation for appointments
- oversee moving a parent from home to a residential community, to an assisted living facility or to a nursing home
- assess the financial, legal and medical situation
- serve as a link between parents and family members
- evaluate all the care options
- take over the role of guardian and/or conservator

Geriatric care managers expect to be paid for their services: normally they charge anything between $50 and $200 per hour (£30-£120). An initial assessment may cost between $150-$350 (£90-£210). Before employing a care manager, various questions need to be asked:

- What services are they offering?
- What are their credentials?

- How long have they been doing this type of work?
- Do they belong to any professional organizations?
- What do they expect to learn from an initial assessment?
- How do they keep in contact with the family?
- How often will they visit the elderly person?
- Can they provide references?
- What are their fees?
- Will they provide a detailed account of their costs?

Lorna P was a retired business woman. She had been married briefly in her early twenties and she had one daughter who was in her early sixties. The daughter lived three hundred miles away from her mother and when Lorna was diagnosed with senile dementia, she employed a care manager to look after her mother's affairs.

The care manager had been recommended by the family lawyer. Lorna's daughter did not like her particularly, but she seemed kind and competent and, after all, she was only being employed in a business capacity. At first the new arrangement ran very smoothly. The courts were happy to accept the care manager as Lorna's conservator. All the bills were paid on time and, when the daughter visited, Lorna seemed happy and well cared for. It was only at the end of the first year, when the care manager submitted her accounts to the court, that the daughter discovered what was happening.

In the first place, the care manager had paid herself more than $30,000 dollars (£20,000)for her services. In addition she had engaged several other people to look after Lorna. Although Lorna was already living in an assisted living facility, the care manager had brought in her own nurse (who happened to be her sister) to conduct a weekly medical examination; she had also employed a team of care assistants to read to Lorna and wheel her about the building. The care manager did not even keep the accounts; she employed an independent book-keeper. Altogether in one year, Lorna's care had cost $160,000 (about £100,000).

Lorna's daughter was furious. She had great difficulty dismissing the care manager because she had been appointed conservator by the courts. In the end she had to give her a substantial severance package and she took over the care management role herself. It was not very difficult; Lorna continued to receive excellent care and the cost dropped by half.

Taking pills

Care must be taken with prescribed drugs. Given that the elderly person may have several chronic conditions, it is important that combinations of drugs do not act adversely with each other. Doctors may give a drug in the generic name, and then another by the brand name. This could cause confusion: patients might think they are two different drugs and thereby take a double dose, when, in fact, they are the same. A further danger is that the elderly may have trouble reading and following the dosage instructions. Problems can also occur if the elderly buy over-the-counter drugs which react negatively with prescribed medication.

To avoid these difficulties, it is necessary to work closely with the doctor. When a new medication is prescribed, a series of questions should be asked:

- What is the generic and the brand name of the drug?
- What is it supposed to do?
- Why has it been recommended?
- How often should it be taken?
- How long should it be taken?
- At what points in the day should it be taken?
- Should food or alcohol be avoided when taking the drug?
- What should be done if a dose is forgotten?
- Are there any possible side-effects?
- How much does it cost? (This does not normally apply in the UK)

When visiting the doctor, the elderly persons should describe:

- The name of all prescription drugs that they take
- The name of any over-the-counter drugs they use
- Any allergies that they have
- Any side-effects they have experienced

When visiting a pharmacy, the same questions should be asked and the same information given.

When taking medication, there are several rules to be followed:

- Don't share medications
- Don't take fewer medications than prescribed
- Keep track of what medications are to be taken
- Ask pharmacists for devices to help remember what medications are to be taken
- Store medications in cool places

If buying medications on the internet, there are several precautions that should be followed:

- Check that the website is a licensed pharmacy in good standing
- Avoid websites that offer to prescribe drugs without a physical examination
- Don't buy from websites that sell drugs without a prescription
- Don't buy wonder drugs

It is clear from the above check-lists, that taking even prescription medicines is a complicated business. If there is any sign of confusion in the elderly person, he or she will almost certainly need careful supervision.

Dealing with dementia

If your parents suffer from dementia, it is necessary to be particularly patient and supportive. You should

- Avoid arguments about forgotten details. Don't say: 'Don't you remember?' (They really don't!)
- Avoid testing parents' memory
- Talk about only one thing at a time

To help the elderly person, it is useful to create reminders and prompts:

- Set aside a place where things are always put such as keys, glasses, a purse, shopping lists, etc.
- Post helpful notes in obvious places such as on the mirror
- Consider what a parent needs when they go out, such as an umbrella – and place it near the door
- Create a place for everything
- Set timers for taking pills
- Make lists
- Put emergency information in one place
- Encourage him or her to retrace steps to remember why he or she went into a room

All her life, Mildred D loved to collect things. Some of her possessions were valuable, but mostly they were sentimental. Once she was in her eighties, her small apartment was full to overflowing. When she began to show signs of confusion, things became very difficult. She was always putting things carefully away 'in a safe place', and then being unable to find them again. As her daughter remarked ,'Mother, you're drowning in things!'

Eventually things got so bad that something had to be done. Reluctantly Mildred agreed that her possessions had to be pruned. She did find the process distressing and her daughter was completely exhausted when the task was finished. However, after a few days, Mildred seemed to have forgotten all the things which had disappeared. A new system was introduced in which particular things were kept in definite places and lists of these places were put up all over the flat. For a time things improved, and the great tidy-up certainly enabled Mildred to stay in her own home longer than would otherwise have been possible.

Offering help

Sometimes elderly people refuse help from their children. What should children do in such circumstances? There are many causes of unwillingness: pride, privacy, self-esteem, the determination not to be a nuisance. However, with tact and diplomacy it is possible to encourage the elderly to accept assistance. Here are some suggestions:

- Take advantage of any complaint by asking questions. Don't inform parents that you suspect a problem; ask if they think they have a problem
- Before suggesting outside help, gather resources so that you can suggest options
- Offer help, but don't give the impression you are taking over
- When parents insist that they don't want to discuss the issue, wait until a better time
- Help parents to accept help by getting someone they respect to recommend it
- Explain how assistance will make them more independent
- Take advice from their friends as to how best to offer help

It is vital that a parent doesn't feel that children are trying to take over their lives. You should ask yourself:

- Do I sound like a parent talking to a child?

- Do I make assumptions about my parents' needs without consulting them?
- Do I make appointments and other arrangements for them without asking them first?
- Do I offer suggestions before asking them what they want?
- Could I be accused of trying to trying to run their lives for them?
- Do I do things for my parents because it is quicker when they could in fact, if I were a little more patient, do them for themselves?

Laura R. had two daughters. The elder had never married and was a successful high school teacher. The younger was far less academic; she was a gentle creature and was the mother of a large family. Because of her lack of domestic responsibilities, it was the elder woman who took the lion's share of Laura's care. She was naturally bossy and had a clear idea how her mother's life should be organized. Laura was equally obstinate in her way and there were frequent battles between them.

It became clear that Laura needed help with personal care and with cleaning. The elder daughter informed her mother of the fact and engaged a suitable helper. Laura promptly fired her. Everyone was at their wits' end. Eventually the younger daughter came to stay for a week. Very gently, she started helping her mother with her daily bath and with organizing the apartment. Laura gradually realized that she liked the new sense of order. Together mother and daughter interviewed several possible aides and it was Laura who made the final decision on which one was to be employed. Although the new aide only came in for an hour every day (Laura flatly refused to pay for more), things ran a great deal more smoothly.

Coping with failing vision

Millions of people over sixty-five suffer from visual impairment. To combat problems with vision, a number of steps can be taken:

- Paint woodwork around doorways in bright colours
- Place extra light on stairs and reading areas
- Distribute light throughout the house
- Check that every room has at least one light that can be turned on by a switch within easy reach of the doorway
- Use night lights
- Encourage the elderly person to take a flashlight with them to read menus in restaurants
- Put a lamp on the table if he or she has difficulty seeing the plate
- Call ahead to reserve a well-lit table if you are taking a parent out for a meal
- Buy a television with a large screen
- Encourage the use of magnifying devices
- Introduce large-print books from the library into the house
- Avoid non-verbal nods and head-shakes, gestures, or smiles. These cannot be seen and therefore do nothing to aid communication

Dealing with deafness

When dealing with those who have a hearing impairment, there are a number of guidelines that should be followed:

- Sit or stand within three feet and face the person
- Make sure your face is in the light
- Understand that some words are more difficult to hear than others
- Enunciate as clearly as possible

- Don't eat while talking
- Keep your hands away from your face
- Point and touch
- Paraphrase
- Use the lower pitches of your voice
- Eliminate TV noise
- Check that hearing aids are working
- Seat the person where he or she can see everyone
- Make sure the person is wearing glasses if necessary
- Announce that you're going to talk about a particular subject

Preserving dignity

Older people can be insecure about their sense of self-worth. It is important that they are always treated with respect. Again there are a number of guidelines:

- You should squat down or pull up a chair so that you are on the same eye-level as an older person
- Try to sit at a good conversational distance
- Ask older people to help with chores
- Show appreciation for their opinions
- Encourage them to make their own choices
- Do not insist on helping them against their will
- Make sure they have enough money for their personal needs

The difficulties of providing care

Unlike professional caregivers, children are expected to be constantly available to help with the problems of care. This can cause a number of difficulties:

- The time spent dealing with elderly parents represents time which is unavailable for spouses and children. This may well be resented. It helps if spouses or children also become involved with the elderly person's care

- Those who care for parents may have the feeling that their work is taken for granted by other members of the family. It is easy to feel unappreciated. Caregivers should consider joining a support group of other carers to discuss their new role

- Caregivers may also feel unappreciated by their parents. Confused elderly people may not perceive how much is being done for them. It is important that those involved in caring share their frustration with someone who can be objective about the situation

- Caring for parents can lead to stress, absenteeism and less efficiency at work. This can lead to resentment. If parents are making excessive demands, it might be helpful to discuss these domestic responsibilities with the boss

- Children who care for parents may also suffer from guilt, feeling that whatever they do is insufficient. It is important to be realistic. If you are doing your best, accept that this is all that can be done

By the time Betty N. reached her late eighties, she needed a substantial amount of care. She was very deaf, but she was also reluctant to wear her hearing aid. She found it difficult to put in; she did not like the way it magnified background noise and she thought the batteries disgracefully expensive. She was also becoming increasingly lame as a result of arthritis in both her hips and her sight was worsening because of slow-growing cataracts.

Betty's own mother had been cared for by Betty when she was old and Betty felt that her daughter should do the same for her. There was also a son, but Betty never expected him to do anything for her, even though he was unmarried and had retired in his mid-fifties. In fact, when he came to visit (which he did faithfully once a week), she tottered into her kitchen to make him coffee and his favourite sandwiches while he watched television. The daughter was a high-powered television executive and she had a husband and three children in higher education. Betty felt that her daughter should give up work. Either she should be invited to live in her daughter's house or, better still, the daughter and her family should move into the same apartment block so that she could be on hand every day. The daughter knew that either alternative would be intolerable and she certainly was not giving up her career.

However, she did the best she could. She visited regularly and she had her mother to stay periodically. She also made sure that there was always food in the house, that her mother's shopping, cleaning and laundry was done and that she continued to see her surviving friends. Nothing was ever enough. Betty complained continually and the daughter suffered endless feelings of guilt.

The caregiver

It is important that children as caregivers recognize the dilemmas and emotional conflicts that may occur as a result of their role. They might think that parents' needs are overwhelming and that their own situation is inconsequential. This is not so. Parent's care can easily expand so that it consumes most of the time and energy of children. Eventually children can feel exhausted, isolated, and resentful. If this happens, they will be of little use. It is therefore necessary to set limits. Children want their parents to be looked after and comfortable, but they should also assess what they can reasonably do. It is necessary to consider the options for care and one's involvement. Once a decision has been made, it should be accepted by all parties. After a system has been established, it should be followed.

Alan O.'s parents were both in their nineties. His mother, aged ninety-three, suffered from senile dementia and had very little idea of what was going on. His father, who was ninety-five, was blind and fairly deaf, but his mind was as acute as ever. Alan had had a very successful career as the headmaster of a famous private school, but was now retired. He and his wife had decided that the old people would be cared for at home. This was partly a financial decision. The cost of a nursing home for both of them would have been phenomenal. Eventually they would have been cared for by the state, but only after their own resources had been exhausted. By looking after them at home, their modest capital could be preserved for the grandchildren. They also believed that the parents would be happier and that they would have a higher standard of care.

Both Alan and his wife were well-educated, highly intelligent people. In cooperation with the doctor and the social services they devised a care plan which covered the old people's needs. However, the strain on them both was enormous. The situation was not helped by the fact that Alan had a younger sister. She had had an equally successful career as a international lawyer and she was also retired. However, she flatly refused to have anything to do with her parents' care. Apart from the occasional telephone call (which the old gentleman could not hear and the old lady could not understand), she had no contact with her parents. When confronted by Alan, she merely shrugged and said that the old people should go into a home. Alan's fury at his sister's attitude was not assuaged by the knowledge that any money left to be inherited was to be divided equally between the two of them.

A number of guidelines should be followed in taking care of the elderly:

- If you are taking care of your parent on a regular basis, you should remove yourself entirely from the situation occasionally. You should take a break for a few hours everyday, or possibly go on a vacation for a few days or a week. While you are away, arrangements can be made for home help

- When caring for a parent, it is vital that your social life is not put on hold. Friends are important in such critical times.

Studies demonstrate that those who have active social lives are better able to cope with the their parents' needs

- When under pressure, caregivers should be careful not to be overwhelmed by circumstances. An attempt should be made to slow down

- Caring for a parent involves constant worry. Rather than fretting at work or lying awake at night, it is best to set a time for worry. If you cannot stop worrying, write down whatever is troubling you and see if you can sort out the problem

- Laughter is vital for both the elderly and for caregivers. Despite the seriousness of geriatric problems, life can still be amusing

- It is vital that caregivers gain perspective about their parents' condition. They should continue to interest themselves in communal activities and world affairs. Similarly, an older person should be helped to see their problems in context. Do whatever you can to help them see beyond their own difficulties

- Inevitably caring for a parent gives rise to disputes with family members, professionals and institutions. When this occurs, caregivers should be assertive. Don't hesitate to ask questions and express your opinions. You should become an educated advocate for yourself and your parents

- Avoid situations where you wish for unrealistic solutions. Try not to focus on what cannot be, and concentrate on practical remedies

- Caregivers should pursue interests beyond the needs of their parents. Hobbies, sports, reading, and socializing are vital

- It may be necessary to have spiritual support in the face of a parents' illness or eventual death. Caregivers should not be afraid of turning to others who can help them

- Under stress, caregivers might be able to use meditation techniques, message or yoga to help them relax. Whatever helps should be pursued

4

Remaining at home

FOR MANY THE most desirable option is to remain at home. If this is possible, various steps need to be taken to ensure that the old people can look after themselves. Independence is crucial, but at the same time it is vital that the elderly can in fact cope with the details of everyday life. There are a number of steps that should be taken to ensure their safety and well-being.

Hilda N. was an independent, determined ninety-year old. She was fairly deaf and a little lame, but otherwise she was remarkable for her age. The thought of an old people's home was abhorrent to her. In any case, she did not think she was old. Nonetheless her children were increasingly concerned about her. She had never been domestic. Her cooking skills were rudimentary and she had never been enthusiastic about laundry and cleaning. It was clear that her apartment was getting dirtier and dirtier; her clothes were beginning to look and smell musty and Hilda herself seemed to be growing thinner. Something had to be done.

Hilda wanted no change. She liked her apartment; her sense of smell was very poor and she had never taken much interest in food. The children would have liked her to go into a home where she would have been properly looked after – after all, she was ninety. Hilda flatly refused. In the end a compromise was reached. It was agreed that the flat must have a professional spring-clean and then a cleaner would be employed to come in once a week. Another aide would be hired for an hour three times a week to give Hilda a bath and to prepare some food for her. Initially Hilda resisted these arrangements. She did not want to spend the money and she did not want any interference in her affairs. But when she realized that her children were serious and the alternative was a residential home, she became reconciled and within six months was grateful for the help.

Safety

Elderly people frequently suffer from bad eyesight, poor balance, impaired hearing and confusion. It is crucial that, if the old person is to stay in their own home, any hazards must be eliminated. The telephone should be programmed to dial an emergency number and a clearly written, large-print list of other important telephone numbers should be put near the telephone. This is important for caregivers as well as for the old people themselves. The list should include police, fire, ambulance, as well as the numbers of family members. It is also useful to add the address of the old person at the bottom of the list in case they become confused. Other steps should also be taken:

- Alert police and fire departments to the fact that an old person is living alone at home
- Make sure that all chemicals, detergents as well as medications are labelled in big letters
- Check that smoke detectors as well as carbon monoxide detectors are working

- Make sure that detectors are located on every floor of the house and outside the bedroom
- Check for escape routes in case of fire. If the old person is in a wheelchair, all doors should be sufficiently wide
- Buy a small fire extinguisher and place in it the kitchen
- Any medical instructions should be taped on a wall in an obvious place
- Ensure that there are two flashlights with working batteries for use if there is a power failure
- Make sure all bathroom and kitchen outlets are working
- Check that the burners in the oven work properly
- Make sure that electrical outlets are not overloaded
- Make sure the hot water does not rise above 120 degrees Fahrenheit
- Since old people get cold, all rooms should be heated adequately

Emergencies

It is important that the elderly person has a medical identification card in his or her wallet that indicates any special medical conditions and lists emergency contacts. It is also advisable to have an emergency response system with a help button which is worn as a pendant or on the wrist. If the old person falls or has chest pains or needs any kind of emergency assistance, the button triggers the telephone to dial a response centre. The centre will then call an emergency number. The old person will then be telephoned, but if there is no response or there is any indication that there is an emergency, a response team will be sent. The price for this system varies: some companies sell the system and then charge a monthly fee; others have a rental service. Some hospitals and social service organizations also offer such systems for free or at a discount to those living on low incomes. Such systems can only work if the old person is able to press the button in a crisis. There may be some instances when this is not possible. If the old person lives alone, it is advisable also to ask neighbours to be on the lookout for any difficulties.

> Kaye B. had always scorned emergency response systems. She used to tell stories of how her friends were always setting them off by accident and that, even when they were set off, no one bothered to telephone to check that everything was all right. As she grew older, she remained independent, but she grew less steady on her feet. One Saturday morning, the telephone rang. She hurried to pick it up and tripped over a chair leg. It was a serious accident. Although Kaye did not know it she had broken her hip. She was a heavy woman and she was unable to move. She was not rescued until Monday morning when her aide arrived to help her with her shower. By this stage she was in a very bad way. She had a mild hyperthermia; she had eaten nothing for two days; she was lying in her own excrement and her hip was to prove very difficult to set. She was taken straight to hospital. Although she did partially recover, she spent the rest of her life in a nursing home.

Crime precaution

The elderly are easy targets for criminals. There are a number of precautions that can be taken:

- Inform the local police that an elderly person is living alone
- Make sure that they can operate their locks easily. If a key is difficult, a coded lock can be used
- Install a peep hole and a security chain in the front door. It should not be opened to strangers unless they can show clear identification or the visitor has previously been invited
- Fix a security alarm system to the house
- Outdoor security lights should also be fitted
- Discuss when it is most sensible for the old person to go outdoors. They should use secure routes to the store or the park

- Valuable jewellery should be left at home preferably in a safe
- Credit cards and money should be carried in an inside pocket or money belt rather than a purse
- Old people should be encouraged to be suspicious of anyone they do not know well.

June R. lived by herself in a small terraced house. When she grew too old to manage the garden, she answered an advertisement in the local newsagent's window. A young man wanted to be employed as a jobbing gardener. She telephoned the number and invited him round to the house. He seemed very pleasant and willing and they arranged that he would start work the following Monday. After they had agreed, she went into the kitchen to make him a cup of tea. Meanwhile he asked to use her bathroom upstairs. They had a nice chat and he left after half an hour. After he had gone, she discovered that £100 ($160) was missing from her dressing table drawer and two diamond rings were also gone. One was her mother's engagement ring. She informed the police who were kind, but held out little hope of their recovery.

Preventing falls

Falls can result in fractures of the hip, spine, pelvis, hand and wrist. Old people may become more sedentary to avoid such dangers. This, however, is a mistake: if the old remain stationary they will have less strength, balance and flexibility and be more apt to fall. Moreover, they will become more isolated and dependent. The best way to prevent falls is by taking exercise such as yoga that helps balance, coordination, and strength.

Home modification

There are various modifications that should be made to the home:

Floors and pathways

- Carpets should be checked for worn areas and tears
- Throw rugs should be discarded
- Nonslip wax should be used on floors
- Hallways should be cleared of footstools, magazine racks, electrical wires and wastepaper baskets
- Hanging plants should be placed at a high level
- Handrails should be put in hallways

Stairs

- Stairs should be avoided if at all possible
- Lifts should be installed if needed
- If stairs are necessary, each step should be no higher than seven inches and deep enough to fit a person's foot
- Handrails should be sturdy and extend the full length of the stairs
- Handrails should be put on both sides of the stairs
- Edges of steps should be marked with coloured, glow-in-the-dark tape
- Nonslip treads should be used on each step

Furniture

- Chairs should be high enough to get out of and into easily
- Chairs should have strong armrests and high backs
- A cane or walker should be located near the chair
- Electric-powered pneumatic chairs that lift up and lower a person should be used if necessary
- The bed should not be too high or low
- Furniture legs that curve outward should be avoided
- Avoid three-legged tables
- Repair any broken or wobbly furniture

Bathrooms and kitchens

- Install grab bars near toilets and bathtubs
- Install a raised toilet seat

- Attach wall-mounted liquid soap dispenser in the shower
- Install nonslip strips or rubber mats on the floor of the bathtub or shower
- Place nonslip strips or rubber bathmats on the bathroom floor
- Put a nonslip rug or rubber mat in front of the kitchen sink
- Avoid bath oils
- Install a shower curtain rather than a glass door

Lighting
- Lights should be bright and distributed evenly
- Light switches should be easy to use and within reach
- Lights should be placed at the entrance to each room and at the top and bottom of stairs
- Install a light by the bed
- Use night lights in the hallway

General matters
- Old people should wear sturdy shoes with low heels. Sandals and shoes with open toes should be avoided. Bedroom slippers should have rubber soles
- Alcohol should be avoided since it affects balance and reflexes
- Temperature should be adjusted suitably
- Items should be organized so that frequently used objects are within easy reach
- Telephones should be put in places where the elderly spend most of their time
- The old should be taught how to get up from chairs and beds with least strain
- Handrails should be placed by the closet
- Old people should be encouraged to use canes or walkers, particularly outside.
- A loose strap should be attached to a cane

Advice for everyday living
If old people want to continue living in their own home, there are

some important changes that should be made to the fabric of the house.

Bathing and grooming
- Handrails should be put in the bathroom and raised toilet seats should be installed
- A chair or stool should be made for the shower area and should be fixed firmly
- Level-style faucets rather than knobs should be installed
- An electric toothbrush should be used
- Various devices should as dental floss holders, wall-mounted soap dispensers, and showerhead attachments should all be fitted

Dressing Room
- Clothes with velcro closures should be used if there is any difficulty with buttons
- The old should wear sweaters that slide easily over the head
- Clothes with zippers rather than buttons should be worn
- Ideally clothes should fasten at the front
- Women should wear dresses with wide necks that slide over the head
- It is preferable to wear clothes that are a size or two larger for ease in dressing
- Old people find silky material or soft knits most comfortable
- Generally an elastic waist has much to recommend it

Lilian Y had always dressed carefully. Even as a very old lady she was elegant in cashmere sweaters and beautifully cut tweeds. Her hairdresser visited her at home every week and she continued to dye her hair an ambitious shade of gold. Her weakness had always been shoes. She was proud of her exquisite small feet and slender ankles and she loved elegant Italian leather shoes with high heels to set them off. Even in her late eighties she had a wardrobe of beautiful shoes. However, walking in them became more and more difficult. She resisted all attempts to persuade her to wear something more practical and by the time she was ninety, she was largely confined to a wheelchair. Although she no longer walked on them, her feet still looked beautiful.

Food

- Seek to discover if there are any difficulties connected with food. Is it hard to go to the grocery store? Is cooking a problem? Are dentures uncomfortable? Is it hard to swallow? Is food simply uninteresting?
- If the old person is unable to go to the grocery store, contact local transportation services to see if a van or volunteer can help Alternatively, organize that food is delivered
- Old people should stock up on frozen and canned foods, pasta, rice, beans, etc once a month
- Small portions of food should be purchased so that unused food is not allowed to spoil
- Old people should be encouraged to buy long-life milk
- When buying prepared food, care should be taken to read labels, looking for food with low sodium and fat content
- Fresh vegetables and fruit should be added to the shopping list
- Carriers should be used when going to the grocery store
- If money is a problem, the elderly should purchase low-cost foods such as rice, dried beans, peas and frozen vegetables. If possible, they should buy food on sale
- Malnourishment is a serious problem among the old. A careful watch must be kept on what is being eaten
- Many areas provide luncheon clubs for old people and in the UK's 'meals on wheels' scheme, volunteers deliver hot nutritious meals to old people's homes. If the old person can be persuaded to take advantage of this, it should be encouraged.

Kitchen

- If old people have stiff joints or weak muscles, there are various aids that can be purchased such as jar openers, lightweight utensils, etc
- Faucet (tap) knobs should be replaced with levers
- If possible, the kitchen should be updated. Small ovens and microwaves are desirable and ideally the old person should never have to bend to get hot food in or out of an oven
- If gas is used in the kitchen, dials should be easy to read
- Utensils, plates, and food should be placed on lower shelves
- Cookbooks with large print and easy recipes should be used
- Packaging should be easy to open
- There should be a fire extinguisher at hand

At the table

- Dining should be a social event if possible. If at all possible old people should have company
- If there is difficulty using knives and forks, they should be longer, thicker and heavier than normal
- Plates should have rims
- Glasses could have built-in straws
- It is better to have food that does not have to be cut up
- Elderly people have less of a sense of smell and taste, so it is useful to use spices and strong flavourings
- Portions should be small
- Dentures should fit properly
- When dining with the family, the old should be encouraged to eat at their own pace
- It is usual for the elderly to eat small portions about six times a day

Swallowing

If swallowing is difficult, the following steps should be taken:
- Several small meals a day should be served
- They should eat sitting up if possible

- Food should be eaten slowly
- Semisolid food should be used
- Thick liquids are easier to swallow
- If the old people are being fed, they should not be hurried

Safety
- You should be aware that the old are particularly vulnerable to salmonella infections
- Meat and eggs should be cooked thoroughly
- When shopping, meat, fish and poultry should be put in separate bags
- Food in cans that are dented should be avoided
- Dates on food should be checked
- Food that is past the expiration date should be thrown out
- All raw food should be washed
- Cut and peeled fruits and vegetables should be stored in the refrigerator
- Kitchen sponges should be changed frequently
- Thaw frozen foods in the refrigerator
- When microwaving, turn the food during the cooking time so it is not undercooked
- Perishable food and leftovers should not be left out for more than two hours
- If food is not eaten immediately, it should be covered
- Large portions of food should be divided and placed into small containers
- The fact that the old person's food is being prepared by an employee does not guarantee that basic rules of hygiene are being followed

Sophie S. was in her late eighties. She was increasingly confused and her children realized that she should no longer be preparing her own food or even living by herself. However, she was determined to stay in her own home, so they found a companion for her to live in the house, to get her up in the morning, to prepare her meals, to take her for a little exercise and to put her to bed at night. Sophie's daughter took a lot of trouble. She interviewed five different women and, although she was expensive, she was satisfied that she had chosen the most suitable candidate for her mother. The companion was a pleasant woman; she had come with good references from her last job as a secretarial assistant and she and Sophie seemed to get on well. However, within three weeks of her companion's arrival, Sophie became ill with sickness and diarrhoea. The doctor was called. He promptly diagnosed food poisoning and, in view of her advanced age, sent Sophie to hospital. When the daughter came to investigate the apartment, she found that the refrigerator was full of out-of-date food and she noticed that the companion did not even wash her hands before starting to prepare lunch. It was obvious what had happened...

Driving

If elderly people still have a car, they should be careful about their driving:

- Eyesight should be tested regularly
- Seatbelts must be worn
- It may be better to disable the airbag
- If the elderly have disabilities such as blurred eyesight, dizziness or confusion, they should be told firmly that their driving days are over
- The car should be in good working order and serviced regularly
- Large mirrors should be installed
- If it is difficult for the elderly driver to see over the dashboard, they should sit on cushions
- Power brakes, steering and seats are desirable
- Trips should be planned in advance
- Driving at night, dawn or dusk should be avoided as well as on unfamiliar routes
- At the first sign of sleepiness, a break should be taken

In most cases, it might be preferable for the elderly to give up driving and use other forms of transportation.

Bernard N was ninety. His wife Beatty was eighty-five. They still lived in their own home and Bernard still had his Jaguar car of which he was inordinately proud. It was a constant worry to all their friends and relations. Beatty suffered from macular degeneration and was disqualified from driving by her eyesight. Bernard had already had one stroke and was not entirely clear in his mind. Driving was a joint operation. Bernard would take the wheel, but he had no idea where to go. Beatty had to tell him where and when to turn. As her sight got worse, it got more and more difficult and frequently they returned home having driven fruitlessly round and round the block. However, they were determined to continue. It got to the point where their son felt he should inform the authorities of his parents' behaviour. In the event, the situation solved itself. Sadly, Bernard had another stroke; he had to be moved to a nursing home and the car was sold. The story could have had a much more unhappy ending with a serious motor accident involving other innocent people.

Home help

If old people continue to live at home, they may well need help. Before determining what level is required, it is important to ascertain exactly what must be done. Is help needed with showering and dressing? Is there a need for someone to do the shopping or cooking for them? Do they simply need a lift to the grocery store? Would a meal delivery service be suitable? Do they need to be taken to the doctor? Is a cleaner needed? Do they need help with finances? After evaluating the situation, you will be able to decide what kind of person is required. There are a variety of options:

Help from family and friends

Family and friends may volunteer to help with the elderly. They certainly should be given small tasks, but it is not fair to expect an adolescent member of the family to take on too much responsibility. Possibly another member of the family will also be needed to supervise such help.

> In her early eighties, Mavis developed Parkinson's disease and went to live in her daughter's house. The daughter worked full-time and much of Mavis's care devolved on the son-in-law who was retired and on her fifteen-year-old grand-daughter. Everyone tried very hard, but the situation was not easy. The grand-daughter in particular was very resentful that she was expected to stay at home sometimes and 'granny-sit' while her friends were out enjoying themselves. The son-in-law was already in his late sixties and found lifting the old lady and pushing her around very taxing. There was a general sense of relief, as well as considerable guilt, when Mavis was admitted into a state nursing home.

Companions

Companions keep the old company, help with minor tasks and generally watch over them. Some companions focus on companionship; others provide assistance. Most companions do not do any housework or chores but they might help prepare a meal, help with dressing, or collect groceries. Companions normally charge from $10-$30 (£6-£20) per hour. Whether they are a success or not depends largely on the kind of people they are. It is vitally important to interview them and to check references.

Homemakers

Homemakers do physical work and socialize less than companions. They do laundry, light housecleaning, prepare meals, and assist with shopping, bathing and dressing. Often they have had special training in the care of the elderly. Homemakers generally charge from $10-$35 (£6-£23) per hour. Again they should be interviewed and references should be carefully checked, preferably by telephone.

> Phoebe was over ninety. She wanted to stay in her own home so her daughter, who lived abroad, contacted an agency which agreed to provide a series of aides to help Phoebe regularly. Although the young man from the agency was most persuasive, the aides were often unsatisfactory. They did not always turn up on time; they were frequently changed; some could not even speak English. Worst of all, when the daughter returned home for a visit, she discovered that all her mother's jewellery had been stolen. Since there had been such a number of aides, there was no means of determining which one had taken it and the young man from the agency disclaimed all responsibility.

Transportation services

If the elderly need a ride to the grocery store, doctor, or day care, it is possible to use transportation services. They charge various fees depending on the service offered.

Care managers

Care managers are usually social workers or nurses with special training in geriatric care. They handle all areas of care including dealing with nursing home staff, home-care workers, community services, financial advisers, etc. Normally a care manager will meet with the old person, with family members, and with others involved in caring. They will assess the old person's abilities and living situation, confer with doctors and formulate a plan outlining what will be done. Care managers usually charge from $75-$250 (£45-£150) per hour. Again it is crucial to check references.

Home health care

Before arranging home health care, the precise needs of the old person must be determined. In general, the following areas should be assessed:

- Meal preparation
- Housework
- Laundry
- Grocery shopping
- Managing money
- Keeping track of medications
- Transportation

If these are the main areas of need, it might be best to hire a homemaker or chore worker. There would be no need for nursing care for these activities. Ideally this level of care will prevent the old person from having to move into full-time residential care. If someone comes in possibly two days a week, this could be sufficient.

At another level of care, the following areas need to be assessed:

- Eating
- Dressing
- Bathing
- Using the toilet
- Getting in and out of bed
- Taking medications
- Getting around the house

If the old person needs help with such activities, a home health care aide who has some training in health care will be advisable. A certified nurse's aide, for example, might be the most appropriate choice. Alternatively, a nurse might be needed. Both registered nurses or licensed practical nurses are able to provide such help. At this level, a doctor would prescribe the kind of care that the old person should receive. Physical therapy, occupational therapy, speech therapy or respiratory therapy might be prescribed.

In selecting a care provider, various guidelines should be followed:

- Describe the old person's condition and ask the aide to describe what he or she would do
- Ask the aide to tell you what training he or she has had for each task
- Ask the aide to show you any certificates or degrees he or she has received
- Ask for a resume that identifies the school the aide attended, previous jobs, and the names of previous employers
- If parents suffer from dementia, discuss what specialized training the aide worker has to deal with this problem
- Ask what training the aide has had in lifting people
- Ask for references and, crucially, take them up

It is useful to interview prospective employees in a neutral place rather than in front of the old person. When you have narrowed the search, invite potential employees to meet the old person and see how they interact. If you hire an aide through a care agency, make sure it is certified. Discover if the aides have been trained and possess qualifications. The following are questions you should ask the agency:

- Is the agency accredited by any professional organization?
- What licenses does the agency have?
- Is the agency insured?

- What services does the agency provide?
- What are the costs?
- Does the agency conduct an initial assessment?
- How does the agency work with doctors?
- Who coordinates care?
- Does the agency operate a 24 hour emergency service?
- Does the agency provide backup if an aide does not come?
- Is it possible to get a replacement for an aide?
- Are there certain things an aide is not allowed to do?

Therapists

Parents may need therapists as well as aides. These are normally recommended by the general practitioner. There are different types of therapists:

- **Physical therapists**: they restore the mobility and strength of patients. Through exercise, massage and equipment they are able to alleviate pain and restore functioning
- **Occupational therapists**: they help patients perform daily activities such as eating, bathing, using the toilet, cooking and dressing. The can asses the house and identify ways to make it more suitable for the elderly
- **Speech language therapists**: they help patients restore speech and also help with breathing, swallowing and muscle control
- **Registered dieticians**: they assist patients in developing a nutritional plan
- **Respiratory therapists**: they evaluate and care for patients with breathing problems

Costs

There are various sources of payment for home health care. In addition to paying for these costs oneself, in the US there is Medicare, Medicade, and medical insurance:

- **Medicare.** This normally covers patients' home health care if they are home bound, under a doctor's supervision, and require medically skilled nursing or therapy. A doctor must prescribe such services. Medical equipment is also covered under Medicare. These services must be part-time.
- **Medicade.** This is a joint state-federal medical assistance programme for individuals on low incomes.
- **Various insurance programmes.** They may cover home health care.

In the UK, the National Health Service provides fairly comprehensive care when it is recommended by the patient's doctor.

5
Daily living

Leaving the house

Assuming that elderly people are still able to live at home, it will be necessary to make adequate arrangements for going out. With planning and patience, they should still be able to deal with the limitations imposed by old age. There are numerous strategies that can be followed to ensure that outings become less of an ordeal.

Planning

In order that outings go smoothly, the following steps can be taken:

- Anticipate what items will be needed, such as medications or a pillow or rug
- Be aware of the old person's limitations as well as your own capabilities
- Telephone ahead to ask questions about the location and size

of bathrooms, stairs, ramps for wheelchair access, etc
- Go over brochures and videos with the old person about the place you plan to visit
- Invite a third person to come to help with the trip
- Don't encourage old people to make difficult trips
- Return to the places that were successful in the past
- Got to know the people you frequently meet on excursions so that they will know the old person's needs

It is important that you go to familiar places; otherwise the elderly may be overcome by anxiety. You should always telephone ahead if special arrangements are needed.

In the last few years of her life, Elsie K. suffered from Parkinson's disease. She was anxious to remain in her own home and her son organized a team of carers to come in to look after her. As she became more infirm, the whole business of daily living became more difficult. Elsie, however, was a courageous and determined person. She had always lived life to the full and she made it clear to her son that, as far as possible, she wanted to continue to do her own shopping, to go to church and to visit her surviving friends. This required a great deal of organisation, but once the routines were established, the carers also enjoyed these regular outings. There is no doubt that they cheered Elsie and helped her become more reconciled to her condition.

When Elsie finally died, her son was amazed at the number of people who came to her funeral in the local church. Largely because of these expeditions, Elsie had managed to keep in touch with a whole range of contacts. When they came to offer their condolences, it was obvious that these people had valued their contact with Elsie every bit as much as Elsie had enjoyed being in touch with them.

Restaurants

If elderly people still enjoy going out to eat, you should make an effort to take them. The experience can be enriched if preparations are made in advance:

- Request a table on the street level so that there is no need to climb stairs
- Make sure that there are no uneven passages in the restaurant
- Ask for a well-lit table
- Find out whether the entry is protected by a canopy or awnings
- Take advantage of 'early bird' dinner specials and senior discounts
- Create new reasons for restaurant outings and family gatherings

Theatres

It is necessary to make arrangements for going to the theatre:

- Order theatre tickets in advance
- Ask the management what accommodation they make for persons with hearing and vision problems
- Ask about the location of toilets
- Go to theatres with elevators
- Request assistance with wheelchairs
- Do not expect ushers to take on extra responsibility for those with physical difficulties
- Seat the elderly person at the end of the row
- Leave the theatre after everyone else has departed

Maeve had always loved the theatre. She had been a pillar of her local amateur dramatic society and her idea of a perfect evening out had always been a visit to a play or musical. When she became very lame with arthritis, she thought that her theatre-going days were over. But her daughter telephoned the local theatre and discovered that there were excellent arrangements for disabled people. Maeve could even see a play without leaving her chair – there was a special place in the auditorium where wheelchairs could be parked for a perfect view of the stage. She also found that, using her hearing aid, she had no difficulty hearing. Maeve's daughter had inherited her mother's love of drama and a monthly visit to the theatre became part of their regular routine. They both enjoyed these trips and the different plays gave them something new to talk about together. There is no doubt that the whole experience enriched their relationship in Maeve's final years.

Travelling

Trips can be difficult for the elderly. Nonetheless, it is possible for parents to get out without difficulties as long as suitable plans have been made:

- Find a travel agent who is prepared to make extensive arrangements for the trip
- Buy travel insurance in case the elderly person is unable to make the trip at the last minute. This may be a problem. Some companies will not insure the very old
- Make sure comfortable shoes are taken
- Ensure that medicine is purchased ahead of the trip
- Make sure that the old person takes medical information with them on the journey including a medical history
- If possible, the old person should wear a MedicAlert bracelet or necklace which is linked to an emergency response

Aeroplanes

When reservations are made for the old, you should inform the airlines that they will need special arrangements. Attempt to avoid surprises by finding out about current security, boarding and baggage reclaiming procedures. Try to avoid air travel at peak times. It is preferable to go to small airports if possible. There are various steps that can be taken to avoid problems:

- Obtain permission to wait with the old person at the gate before boarding
- Ask for a private screening at security if the old person needs assistance
- Request a tram ride from the security area to the gate
- Order a wheelchair if necessary
- Request seating near the bulkhead
- Pack drugs which are needed for the trip in a carry-on bag
- Request a seatbelt extender
- Request a seat close to the toilet at the front of the plane
- Pack a snack, a blanket and a neck pillow
- Ensure that the old person wears compression stockings and does stretching exercises during the trip

When Isabel was in her eighties she had severe diabetes; she was overweight and was largely confined to a wheelchair. However, she longed above all things to pay a visit to her twin brother. He had had several heart attacks and was resident in a nursing home in Florida. Isabel lived in a suburb of Philadelphia. The air companies were not encouraging, but eventually Isabel found one carrier who was willing to fly her to Miami provided that she was accompanied and provided that she flew entirely at her own risk. Isabel was willing to take the chance and she took a younger friend with her who was a trained nurse.

The whole expedition was a great success. Brother and sister were able to sort out old misunderstandings and they had a very happy weekend together. When they said good-bye, they kissed with real affection. They knew they were not likely to see each other again. The return journey went equally smoothly and two months later Isabel heard that her twin had died. For the rest of her life she was glad that she had been able to make that one final effort.

Ships

Cruises are especially good for the elderly because everything is provided on board including restaurants and entertainment as well as medical assistance. Some ships also provide wheelchair access. There are a number of questions you should ask in advance:

- Is the ship suitable for those using wheelchairs?
- Is casual dining available?
- What is required for shore excursions?
- Are there likely to be queues for dining or evening events?
- Is there a small number of passengers so that socializing is possible?
- Is it necessary to board small boats to go on shore?
- Are there special policies for travellers with disabilities?
- Are activities available when the ship is in port?

Trains

Going by train is also a possibility, but it is desirable to check about a number of factors:

- Can the train accommodate wheelchairs?
- Are refreshments brought to travellers?
- Are toilets suitable for the elderly?
- Is there a long distance between where tickets are sold and the point of departure?
- Are conductors available if needed on the journey?

Old people should always take mobile telephones with them in case they need to make calls on the trip. It is also sensible to see if discounts are offered for senior citizens.

Buses

It is common for community groups to arrange outings by bus to botanical gardens, museums and historic sites. Often discounts are given for the elderly. You should make sure that mobility problems are catered for. When making bookings, be sure to tell the company about the old person's special needs. Again they should be encouraged to take a mobile telephone with them in case they need to make a call.

Cars

If the old person is ever to go out, it is necessary that they use a car if at all possible. Getting in and out can present difficulties for old people and their caregivers. The following strategies should be employed:

- Place a piece of plastic on the seat before the old person gets in to make sliding in and out easier
- Tell the old person to get in the car bottom first
- They should put feet out first when leaving
- Use a small seat cushion to raise the old person up to give them a better view
- Carry a step stool to help them climb in and out of minivans
- Make sure that the driver has a mobile phone in case it is necessary to make a call
- Ensure that the seatbelt is worn
- Put a sign for the handicapped in the window when parking and park as close to the destination as possible

Depression

One of the most important reasons to encourage outings and little trips is to provide variety and to avoid depression. Daily living can be difficult for the elderly, but there are many strategies for keeping depression at bay:

- Keep a list of favourite activities and ask them to choose what they would like to do
- Organize a visit from someone who lifts their spirits
- Arrange an outing
- Get the old person up and moving. A regular walk outdoors is recommended if the weather is fine
- Appeal to the child inside every older person. Prepare a soothing bath, read a story, watch a comedy on video
- Ask for help with a task the old person is good at
- Request help with shopping, gardening, drying dishes, etc
- Encourage activities that stimulate self-expression

Louise B had always been subject to depression. Her friends at school used to call her 'Eeyore' because she always saw the gloomy side to any situation. When she became old and rather deaf, this tendency became more pronounced. She felt that she was useless; that she was a nuisance to her children; that there was nothing to look forward to and that really she would be better off dead. Her three daughters did their best to stimulate her and to provide little treats to which she could look forward. This strategy was not unsuccessful, but it was very exhausting for the daughters. Then they hit upon the idea of buying her a computer. Louise insisted that she was far too old to learn new skills, but, with the help of a computer-literate grandson, she soon got the hang of it. She was soon sending out e-mails to all the members of the family; she spent hours looking up things that interested her; she became a habitué of various chat rooms (her daughters were not sure they approved of this); she used the desk-top publishing facility for making all her own Christmas and birthday cards and she adored buying things on on-line auctions. Her daughters started joking that she would soon need a bigger flat!

Clinical depression

Clinical depression can continue for weeks or even months. It disturbs sleep, appetite and the quality of an old person's life. It can seriously affect health. Some people have an inherited disposition to such depression. There are a number of signs:

- Feeling hopeless, sad or frightened
- Showing lack of interest in everyday activities
- No longer enjoying pleasurable pursuits
- Crying for no apparent reason
- Complaining of lack of concentration
- Having a faulty memory
- Expressing feelings of worthlessness or guilt
- Having thoughts of suicide
- Complaining of headaches, backaches or stomach aches
- Using more alcohol or drugs
- Sleeping too little or too much
- Appearing tired
- Eating more than usual
- Frequently becoming hostile or disoriented
- Adopting depressive postures

It is important to discover causes of depression. It can be triggered by an upsetting event or series of events such as moving to a new place, having financial problems, coping with a disease, or undergoing stress. Worry and loneliness can also be contributory factors. To combat depression, it is sometimes helpful to encourage the old person to reminisce about the past. It can help to recast events by highlighting positive features of previous experiences. By reflecting on the past, the old person can counter depressive feelings and can remind themselves of previous roles as fathers and mothers, teachers, etc. Such a life review can bring into focus the constructive actions they once took in to help their children, friends and the community. It is therapeutic for parents to write autobiographies for other family members, or to produce a journal consisting of photos, letters, postcards, greeting cards, sketches and poetry. An alternative approach to countering depression is to encourage the old to participate in support groups, become volunteers, and stay involved with the local community.

> When Rebecca V. stopped caring about her appearance, seemed to eat very little and complained of constantly waking up in the middle of the night, her son was worried. He insisted that she go to the doctor to discuss the situation. The doctor diagnosed clinical depression and put her on a short course of anti-depressants. Initially they seemed to have no effect, but after a few months she seemed to revert to her old busy self. All the family rallied around to make sure she had plenty of stimulation and, after half a year, the whole episode was forgotten. Rebecca's son was always glad that he had insisted on the doctor's visit as soon as he noticed something was wrong. Things could have been much worse if the depression had been allowed to take greater hold.

An important step in countering chronic depression is to take medication. The following are the most common types of drugs prescribed for depression:

- **Tricyclic antidepressants**. These drugs can cause weight gain as well as sedation. Doctors have to be careful in prescribing and monitoring them because older individuals are prone to adverse side-effects, including increased heart rates, confusion, constipation and decreased blood pressure
- **Selective serotonin reuptake inhibitors**. These medications produce fewer adverse side-effects. They are safer for those

who have both a physical disorder and suffer from depression
- **Monoamine oxidasle inhibitors.** These medications are not usually prescribed. They require stringent dietary restrictions and special precautions.

Anxiety

Anxiety occurs when worrying or nervousness is intense. Sometimes it is temporary, but it can be a very disabling condition. There are various forms:

- **Generalized anxiety disorder.** This affects about 5 to 7 per cent of the elderly and is more common in women. It is characterized by months of constant, exaggerated worrying thoughts and being sure that the worst will occur
- **Phobia.** This anxiety is marked by intense irrational fear of something that poses little or no real danger
- **Panic disorders.** Sufferers experience repeated episodes of intense fear. It can result in chest pain, heart palpitations, shortness of breath, dizziness, abdominal pain, feelings of unreality or fear of dying
- **Obsessive-compulsive disorder.** This is identified by repeated, unwanted thoughts or repetitive behaviour such as checking over and over that, for example, doors are locked or that necessities are not forgotten
- **Post-traumatic stress disorder.** This can occur after a specific disaster. It can result in persistent nightmares, flashbacks, numbing of emotions, depression and irritability.

It is important to point out that not all feelings of anxiety are irrational. As we have already seen, the old are too often vulnerable to criminals. Their health can be precarious; they may be dependant on their children or on professional carers for their everyday survival and all too often they are lonely and deprived of human contact.

However, if any of the following symptoms of anxiety persist, it is sensible to visit the doctor:

- Agitation
- Irritability
- Apprehension
- Rapid heartbeat
- Uncomfortable awareness of heart rate
- Shortness of breath
- Fainting or dizziness
- Upset stomach
- Nausea
- Diarrhoea
- Frequent urination
- Exaggerated response when startled
- Extreme watchfulness
- Insomnia
- Concentration difficulties

Jessica L lived by herself in sheltered accommodation. If there was an emergency, there was a panic button and a warden was on duty from nine until five on weekdays. Nonetheless Jessica saw very few people. She was eighty-nine years old; she had been a widow for twenty years and most of her friends were dead. She did not particularly like her neighbours and, in any case, contact was difficult. She was very deaf and she was not inclined to wear her hearing aid. She did have one daughter, but she was a corporate lawyer and she lived in a city five hundred miles away.

The daughter made the effort to visit her mother twice a year. Ten years previously, they had discussed Jessica moving nearer, but Jessica had always maintained that she was happy where she was. She did not want to be a burden and, at that stage, she still had friends living nearby. Nothing seemed to change, but, on one visit, the daughter noticed that her mother had suddenly become far more anxious. She seemed convinced that she was vulnerable;

she insisted on double-locking her doors at all times and she was clearly frightened. The daughter made some enquiries, but could find no solid reasons for her mother's feelings. There had been no break-ins in the complex and she had not had a bad experience when she was out shopping.

The daughter insisted that Jessica consult the doctor. After a long chat, he told the two women that he believed that these feelings were engendered from watching too many alarming programmes on the television. Jessica was spending too much time alone. Something had to change. Jessica was persuaded to move into Assisted Living accommodation in a facility near her daughter's house. The move was a nightmare and it took a little time for Jessica to settle, but, by the time she celebrated her ninetieth birthday things were back on an even keel; the daughter and her family visited frequently and the anxiety had completely disappeared.

There are various remedies for anxiety. Milder forms can respond to pleasurable activities. Music can also help as does walking outdoors. The following can also help:

- Relaxation training. Patients are taught how to let go of muscle tensions
- Meditation. This can reduce high blood pressure and slow the heart rate
- Prayer. This can be of considerable benefit

Cognitive-behaviour therapy can help replace anxious thoughts with more realistic ones in potential catastrophes so that elderly people can react differently in situations that cause anxiety. The old can also learn to relax while exposed to fearful objects or situations. In some cases it may help to undergo drug treatment. Such medications have few side effects.

Improving relationships

Dealing with an older person can be fraught with difficulties for both the elderly and the caregiver. Both can feel a range of emotions including love, hurt, disappointment, sadness and hope. Yet, it can be a time to seek to improve relationships. There are a number of techniques for doing this:

- Ask the older person about the past
- Inquire about childhood and youth
- Be curious about how they spent their time at work
- Create special times to be together such as during meals
- Hold an older person's hand
- Bring gifts
- Refrain from criticizing annoying habits
- Wait for the person to finish speaking during a conversation
- Indicate that you are interested
- Ask for details about what you are told
- Summarize to indicate that you heard what is said
- Ask questions
- Refrain from expressing anger over past events
- Don't expect an older person to change
- Recognize that you may not always agree
- Try to be forgiving
- Attempt to understand an older person's motives
- Accept that you may never be close

Judith L had never been close to her daughter. Always a 'Daddy's girl', the daughter felt that her mother had neglected the family in the pursuit of her career as a social worker. There was little sympathy between the two women. The daughter was intensely domestic and family-orientated. She had put all her energies into being a good mother and she bitterly resented the neglect that she had been subject to during her own childhood.

When Judith became old, she longed to have her daughter visit and look after her. She was lonely and she could not understand why her daughter was not more willing to spend time with her. By this stage her memory was growing hazy, but she did know she had spent most of her time looking after people. In view of this, she could not imagine that she had been anything but an excellent mother.

The daughter was mature enough to realize that there was no point in explaining her reluctance to her mother. Judith would never believe it and it would only make her more unhappy. The solution was to establish a routine that was tolerable for both of them. Happily there was enough money to employ aides for all the day-to-day matters. The daughter visited every Sunday and gave her mother her lunch. During these sessions Jessica was encouraged to talk about her professional life and her more interesting cases. Family matters were avoided. Over the weeks, the daughter grew to admire her mother. She continued to feel anger at how she was neglected as a child, but she saw that her mother did have some very admirable qualities and, in many ways, had had a very successful life.

In supporting the elderly, it is important to deal with potent emotions. It is frequently the case that caregivers feel guilt and a sense of helplessness. It is vital to come to terms with these feelings. Children should attempt to ascertain how much they are realistically prepared to do for their elderly parents. They should not feel guilty for doing too little in the face of overwhelming demands. Instead, they should make a list of what they are honestly proposing to do such as provide emotional support, talking with doctors and caregivers, look for a nursing home, help with financial problems and ensuring that parents will be properly looked after. It is vital to set limits and then do what is practical.

Visiting the hospital

It is usual for the elderly to experience hospital care even if they live at home: 50 per cent of those over 80 enter a hospital every year. Given this expectation, it is important for older individuals to have an understanding of what is involved in a hospital visit. No matter how congenial they may appear, hospitals are frightening, especially to those facing physical difficulties.

In Britain, patients are recommended by general practitioners to see specialists who arrange for hospital care. The National Health Service provides comprehensive facilities for all ailments, and patients are treated at local hospitals where specialists deal with specific problems. Those who have health insurance have greater choice, and can go to private hospitals. In the US, on the other hand, there is no similar governmental health service. Patients are free to select specialists without the recommendation of general practitioners. However, doctors can only work in hospitals where they have admittance privileges. This limits the choice that patients can make of the hospitals in which they will be treated. In addition, Medicare plans or private insurance policies might require that patients go to doctors and hospitals within a certain network.

Despite these restrictions in both countries, there may be opportunities to select both doctors and hospitals that specialize in various fields. Generally large medical centres associated with a university have high calibre specialists, dedicated clinics and sophisticated technology. The disadvantage of such institutions is that patients might get less attention and care than in smaller hospitals. An important point to consider is that teaching hospitals train young doctors, and use patients as teaching models. This can cause considerable distress as well as embarrassment for the elderly. In the US, Veteran Affairs hospitals are sometimes overwhelmed by bureaucracy, but they can also be associated with university hospitals, hence the care is of a high standard. Of course in emergencies patients may have to go to the nearest hospital, but they can be transferred to the hospital of their choice later.

Entering a hospital

When an older person enters a hospital, a range of information will need to be available including name, address, phone number, birth date, next of kin, as well as health insurance. In the US, the Social Security, Medicare, and Medicade numbers are also required. Hospitals will also need to know what medications an older person takes, what allergies they have, and information about previous injuries and hospitalization. Among the forms that will need to be signed is a consent form which states that the hospital is permitted to do whatever is required for the patient. The staff need a patient's consent before undertaking any measures beyond emergency precautions. Most hospitals will not admit patients unless they sign this form. It is helpful to fill out such forms in advance if you know hospitalization is likely to be necessary.

If possible, you should ask if there is a choice of room. If there is an option, it would be best to have a bed near a window: natural light and a view can be beneficial for the elderly. You should also ask about privacy and anything else that is worrying the elderly person. You might also request information about a telephone and a television as well as newspaper delivery, internet access, books and magazines. When packing for a stay in hospital, you should include:

- Hearing aids, glasses, dentures, and a cane or walker
- A supply of medications along with a list of medications, dosages, as well as allergies
- Copies of legal documents
- Slippers
- Socks
- Pyjamas
- Robe or nightgown
- Toothbrush, toothpaste, soap, deodorant, shampoo, and razor
- Clock
- Ear plugs

- Portable radio
- Portable television
- Mobile telephone
- Small amount of cash

Tests and surgery

Particularly in the US, doctors tend to overprobe and overscan older people because they are fearful of malpractice lawsuits. This can be distressing. Yet, it is important that appropriate tests and treatments are carried out. To ensure that this is done, you should ask questions, make informed decisions, and get second opinions if necessary. In the US, Medicare, Medicaid or other insurance will cover the costs of a procedure as well as other expenses. Questions that might be asked are:

- Why is this test or treatment recommended?
- How long will it take?
- What is the likely recovery time?
- Is surgery absolutely necessary?
- What will the test reveal?
- What are the risks involved?
- What other options are there?
- How much will it cost?

Lydia S was in her eighties and was suffering from a slow-growing cancer which was likely to be terminal. Once she was admitted to hospital the doctors put her through a battery of tests. Lydia found these distressing and exhausting. As a trained nurse, she had no illusions about her condition. She persuaded her son to talk to the doctors to explain that what she wanted was palliative care. She accepted that she was going to die and she wanted the process to be as easy and painless as possible. Once the son had explained the situation, everything went much better. It was decided that

Lydia did not really need a hospital at all and would be better off in a cancer-care hospice for the terminally ill. The last month of her life was a very happy time for all concerned.

In a hospital the doctor will oversee a patient's medical care, but nurses are crucial. They are the ones who notice if a medication is having bad side-effects, if an older person has new symptoms, or if there are significant changes. When dealing with nurses, you should:

- Show respect
- Ask questions
- Provide information
- Offer to help with tasks
- Treat nurses with kindness

Visits

When you go to visit an elderly person in the hospital, you should:

- Be polite and unobtrusive
- Prepare in advance for the visit
- Arrange for privacy
- Respect the rules
- Have physical contact with the patient if appropriate
- When taking children, make sure they are well-cared for and do not disturb other patients

6

Financial planning

C ARE FOR THE elderly can be costly. Thus, it is vital to assess the financial assets of older people and make realistic choices. It is not uncommon for older individuals to be fearful of running out of money. In addition, children may be worried about the soaring costs of medical care and nursing homes. All of these issues require careful financial planning and the monitoring of expenses.

Dorothy C. was the widow of a businessman. He had done well and Dorothy was left comfortably off. She had been a teenager in the 1930s and the experience of her parents losing all their savings in the Depression still haunted her. She had always been careful with money and as she grew older, this characteristic intensified. Her children urged her to turn the heating up, to take taxis when she wanted to go somewhere and to go out to eat whenever she felt like it. Dorothy felt all these things were unnecessary extravagances.

She fell and broke her hip. When she came back from hospital, it was obvious that she needed help with personal care and with looking after her flat. She was very reluctant to hire anyone and when her children insisted, she would only accept one hour's help three times a week. When questioned, she said that she had to be careful and save 'for a rainy day.' When her children pointed out that she was ninety and that perhaps it was now raining, she took no notice.

It became clear that she really needed residential care. Her daughters found a very nice nursing home, but Dorothy flatly refused even to go to see it. When she was told how much it cost, she declared that she could not afford it. Eventually, senile dementia set in and she did spend the last two years of her life in the nursing home, but by that stage she did not know where she was. When she died her children discovered that she was worth nearly £2,000,000 ($3,500,000). It was all invested in low interest government bonds and, because she had done no estate planning, much of it was lost in death duties.

Discussing finances

When the elderly are facing difficult decisions about care, it is necessary to assess their situations realistically. At the very least documents must be found and be kept in a safe place. Because money is a private affair, you should be tactful. Older individuals may be reluctant to disclose their financial situation; they may resist advice. It is important to consider the situation from an older person's perspective. This may prove difficult because people who were born in the prosperous 1950s and 1960s tend to have very different financial attitudes from those who grew up in the Depression years of the 1930s. Those who experienced the Depression watched prices rise astronomically; there was job insecurity and widespread poverty. There are other difficulties. Some elderly people simply do not want anyone to know about their situation. Possibly, they are embarrassed about the way money has been mismanaged in the past. Further, they may feel afraid of losing control over the estate. These possible difficulties should not inhibit the exploration of an older person's financial situation. It is vital that financial planning is instituted to protect the elderly from future financial distress.

> John A had always been secretive about money. He saw himself as the family breadwinner and even his wife had no idea how much he earned. After he became a widower, he continued to live modestly and confided in no one about his financial affairs. When John showed signs of Alzheimer's disease and needed to go into a nursing home, his children had no idea what kind of facility could be afforded. They had the greatest difficulty persuading him to give them power of attorney and it took them a long time to trace all his accounts and discover the true situation. It turned out that he was not well-off at all. He had apparently lost a lot of money in an unwise business venture and was so ashamed that he had never told anyone. As a result, he had never claimed for a whole range of government social benefits to which he would have been entitled and which would have made his old age more comfortable.

Financial planning

Regardless of the size of an elderly person's estate, he or she should do some financial planning to avoid a crisis. A financial plan can be formal and comprehensive, or it can simply consist of reviewing one's worth, establishing an income, and organizing a budget. It is vital that a strategy be established to pay for future expenses and care. If there is a relatively large estate, it will be necessary to review investments and insurance, and to consider how to protect assets from tax and possibly estate duty. Those with smaller estates in the US might look into low-income benefits and eligibility for Medicade. There are similar benefits for the less well-off in the UK. The budget planner listed below will help to make a start:

Assets
House and other real estate
Cars, boats, and other property
Valuables
Checking current accounts
Savings accounts
Stocks, bonds and mutual funds
Annuities
Trusts
Life Insurance
Loans
Equity in a business
Other

Debts
Mortgages
Outstanding loans
Outstanding debts
Outstanding bills
Credit cards
Other

Income
Salary
Business income
Pensions
Social Security
Dividends
Interest from investments and savings
Rental Income
Other Social Benefits

Current expenses
Mortgage or rent
Taxes

Utilities
Food
Travel
Vacation travel
Clothing
Medications
Medical costs
Insurance
Home maintenance
Housekeeping
Home care
Interest payments
Hobbies
Pets
Entertainment
Gifts
Donations
Other

Future expenses
Nursing Home
Residential Home
Home health care
Assisted Living
Medical bills
Sheltered Accommodation

After planning a budget, the elderly should be encouraged to calculate their net worth. Ideally a list should be made of all assets including savings, investments, real estate, etc., and then calculate their debts including mortgages, loans, bills, etc. The net worth of individuals will provide a framework to plan for the future. It may be necessary to adjust the budget so that there is no overspending, and the budget may need to be altered as the total estate decreases. Another possibility is to eliminate some areas of expenditure, or possibly tap into other sources of income such as a home that can be used as collateral against a loan, a life insurance policy that can be cashed in, or the sale of another property. It is important to consider possible nursing care costs and their impact on an estate. In creating a financial plan, it is necessary to discuss goals and priorities and to have a realistic assessment of the individual's financial strengths and weaknesses. Financial plans should be reviewed at regular intervals, and if there are any major changes in circumstances.

> Rosemary S. was very vague about money. She had been left adequately well off by her doctor husband, but before he died she had had nothing to do with the family accounts. For the first time, at the age of eighty, she had to face up to managing money. With the help of her daughter, she bought a large account book and listed all her assets. She was pleased to discover there were very few debts – the mortgage had been paid off long ago and she had never had a credit card. Then she kept a careful account of all her income (state pension, private pension and dividends) and all her expenditures. After the first year she was relieved to discover that she was living comfortably within her income. She could afford to give a generous wedding present to her favourite grand-daughter and she knew that, when the time came, she could afford to go to a first-class nursing home. Once it was all sorted out and the situation became clear, Rosemary became far more relaxed as a person. She was always grateful to her daughter for insisting that she faced up to reality.

To simplify matters, it might be sensible to:

- Consolidate all accounts and place them into one financial institution
- Consider selling real estate beyond an elderly person's home
- Paying bills automatically through direct debit facilities or similar
- Ensure that pension cheques and social security monies are deposited automatically

Benefits and discounts

It is helpful to find out what services and discounts are available for the elderly. Often money is spent unnecessarily. In addition to Medicare and Medicade in the US, there are various types of health-care cover and insurance policies. Social security also provides income to workers past retirement. It is useful to go online to look for any sources of revenue that can help with health care. Even for those who are financially secure, there are programmes that can lower bills or provide for services. For those on low incomes, there is the possibility that governmental facilities will be available.

The areas to look for discounts and special services include:

- Grocery stores that provide free deliveries as well as senior discount days
- Veterinarians who provide discounts and pet-walking services
- Pharmacies that offer free deliveries
- Hairdressers who make house calls
- Phone and utility companies that offer discounts as well as other services
- Local power and gas companies or energy agencies that offer discounts and other services
- Local power and gas companies as well as energy agencies that help insulate and weather-proof homes
- Health care clinics, hospitals and public health departments that provide special free services
- Dentists and hygienists who provide discounts and services for the homebound
- Restaurants that offer discounts at certain times
- Supplementary Security Income is also available in the US for elderly people on limited incomes
- Food stamps in the US are designed to promote the welfare of those on low-income
- In the US, the government's Low Income Home Energy Assistance Program helps pay energy bills while in the UK,

pensioners are given a lump sum towards winter heating bills
- All local telephone companies are required to join Link-Up-America which helps cover the cost of installing a new phone. Lifetime Assistance covers the cost of monthly bills

Mortgages

It is possible to borrow money using one's home as collateral. By refinancing the house or getting a second mortgage, funds can become available for various needs. A reverse mortgage can also provide a lump sum of cash for renovating the house or paying ongoing bills. Unlike other types of loans, they do not have to be repaid until the sale of the house or death of the borrower. Because of this there are no income qualifications or monthly payments. Moreover, closing costs and fees are usually financed within the mortgage. All that is necessary is for the old person to pay his usual taxes, insurance, and the cost of maintenance or repair.

In the US, federal insurance plans, known as Home Equity Conversion Mortgages, are widely available. They are provided by private lending institutions but backed by the government. The elderly are allowed to remain at home as long as necessary. Payments are guaranteed in case the lender defaults. Such mortgages are usually less expensive and offer larger cash advances than other similar loans. To receive this type of loan, the house must be the primary residence and at least a year old.

Privately backed reverse mortgages are not insured by the government, but are privately sponsored. These are generally more expensive but useful if the house is valuable. Uninsured loans are not insured by the government and have fixed terms. The loan must be paid back on a predetermined date. Such loans are useful if money is needed for a specific period of time and there is an expectation that the house will be sold before or at the end of the term. Home repair loans, which are normally offered by government housing agencies, provide a one-time lump sum for home repairs. They are offered without interest or at a very low rate.

It is important to stress that before embarking on any of these schemes, professional, independent advice should be sought. In the UK these schemes have been associated with serious scandals and by embarking on them some old people have found themselves very much worse off.

Martin S, at the age of eighty-three, was finding it increasingly difficult to live on his income. However, he still lived in a very pleasant house in a good area and he wanted to continue to do so. He discussed the matter with his children and they encouraged him to look into a home equity loan. After examining what was on offer and consulting an independent financial accountant, he took out a loan. This made all the difference to his standard of living and it made his final years considerably more comfortable.

Professionals

There are various types of financial experts:

- Financial planners specialize in financial planning. Most have qualifications
- Accountants handle taxes and auditing. Most are certified public accountants
- Lawyers deal with estates, wills, and trusts
- Brokers buy and sell stocks and bonds

Health Care

Health Care, particularly in the US, is expensive. The following are some of the various options available.

- Medicare is a federal health insurance for those over 65. It

covers most medical and hospital care
- Medical Advantage offers the same or more coverage than Medicare, but often limits care to a specific group of doctors and hospitals
- Medigap is an additional policy which covers some areas not covered by Medicare
- Employee or retiree coverage is health care covered by a former employer
- Military benefits are provided for veterans
- Prescription drug coverage is provided as a plan by Medicare
- State programmes help those on limited incomes pay for Medicare.
- Medicade is a governmental health insurance programme for those on low incomes.
- Federally qualified health centres offer low-cost health care
- Long term insurance care covers nursing homes
- Pace provides full medical and daily care for very frail elderly individuals living in the community
- Waiver programmes are provided by States that sue Medicaid funds to offer various services that are not usually covered under Medicaid
- Continuing Care Retirement Communities are full care residences which are normally private and expensive. Some are charitable foundations which also provide for the indigent

Medicare

Medicare is the main federal health insurance in the US for people over 65 and certain disabled people under 65. Anyone who receives social security benefits gets a Medicare card when they are 65. Medicare allows persons to choose the Original Medicare Plan, or a variety of other plans called Medicare Advantage. Those who choose this option are still covered under Medicare. In most cases they also receive additional coverage for certain tests, exams and medical services. However, they may be limited in the choice of a doctor.

The basic Medicare Plan is divided into two parts. Part A is hospital insurance; Part B is medical insurance. Part A covers most hospital bills, hospice care and limited nursing home and home care. Part B is medical insurance which covers most doctors' fees, medical equipment, and outpatient care. Most people pay a monthly premium of about $70 which is taken directly out of social security. An annual deduction of about $100 must be met before payments begin. After this the enrolee pays a share of the cost of any service. Part B is optional. If an older person receives social security, that individual is enrolled automatically.

Marjorie B. was the only daughter of affluent mid-Western parents. She was never encouraged to follow any form of career. After school she studied music and then it was thought she would get married. In fact this never happened. She merely stayed at home looking after her parents and then, after their deaths, interested herself in cultural activities. She did not have a good financial advisor and over the years her capital and also her income diminished. By the time she was in her mid-eighties, she found it quite difficult to manage. Her friends were horrified to discover that because she had never worked, she had no social security entitlement and, worse still, no Medicare. This meant that if she ever became ill, she would have to pay for all health care privately.

Marjorie's friend Ruth W. grew up in similar circumstances. Her father was shrewder than Marjorie's. Like Marjorie, Ruth helped her parents round the house and occasionally acted as her father's secretary. However her father insisted on formally employing her and, instead of giving her an allowance, he paid her a salary. She therefore had a record of social security contributions and when she was old she was entitled to the full range of Medicare benefits.

Medicare Advantage offers services beyond Medicare. Private insurance companies have contracts with Medicare. They often offer broader coverage but limit which doctors and hospitals can be used.

Medicare Advantage is of four types:

- **Managed Care.** Under this plan, older persons can only go to doctors and other carers who are on the plan's network. Also, the person's primary-care doctor may have to make a referral in order for a specialist to be seen.
- **Preferred Provider Organization.** This is much like managed-plans except that people can see specialists without referrals from a primary doctor.
- **Private Fee-for-Services.** These plans are similar to the Medicare Plan except that a private company, rather than Medicare, determines the approved fees, premiums, deductibles, and co-payments. The elderly can go to any doctor or hospital that is approved by Medicare.
- **Speciality Plan.** These plans provide normal Medicare coverage plus any extra care that is needed because of a particular disorder.

The following represent what is covered and not covered in Medicare:

Medicare Part A Hospital Insurance
Hospital stays: The first 60 days are covered; the next 30 days require a co-payment. Co-payments beyond 150 days, private nurses, the extra cost of private rooms and television and telephone are not covered.
Nursing home care: Skilled care that follows a hospital stay of at least 3 days, the first 30 days in a benefit period, medication and meals are covered. However, co-payments and costs beyond 100 days in a benefit period, custodial care, care not related to a hospital stay of 3 days or more, and extra charges for a private room are not covered.
Home health care: Part-time or skilled care which is prescribed by a doctor for treatment or rehabilitation are covered; custodial care is not covered.
Hospice care: All medical and nursing care, medical supplies, home

care, counselling, short-term hospital or respite care, drugs for pain and symptoms are covered.

Psychiatric care: 190 days in a psychiatric hospital is covered; ongoing care over 190 days is not covered.

Blood: All but the first three pints are covered; the first three pints in each year are excluded.

Medicare Part B Medical Insurance

Doctors Fees: Most bills from doctors are covered; however, charges in excess of approved fees, routine examinations and routine dental care are not covered.

Outpatient care: Most medical services and supplies are covered.

Therapy: Medically necessary outpatient physical, occupational and speech therapy are covered and there is no limit if therapy is provided by a hospital outpatient facility.

Diagnostic and laboratory services: Blood and urine tests, X-rays, scans, and screening are covered.

Medical equipment and supplies: Hospital beds, wheelchairs, oxygen supplies, and walkers are covered; glasses, hearing aids and dentures are not covered.

Ambulance service: Cost of ambulance transport is covered.

Preventative care: Mammograms, pap smears, and pelvic exam, pneumonia, hepatitis B, and flu shots; bone mass, colorectal, prostate, heart disease, and glaucoma screening are covered. Most other preventative care is not covered.

Drugs: There is coverage for a few prescriptive drugs; most prescriptions are not covered.

Blood: All but the first three pints; the first three pints in each calendar year.

Medigap

Medigap is a private health insurance, separate from Medicare. It supplements Medicare and pays the cost of premiums, deductibles and physician bills that exceed Medicare's approved charges. Medigap insurance protects people from ongoing medical expenses. However, it is not designed for those enrolled on Medicare Advantage Plan or other heath group plans that provide wide coverage. The benefits include:

- Co-payments for hospitalization
- Coverage for 365 additional days beyond Medicare's hospital benefits
- Co-payments required under Part B of Medicare
- First three pints of blood each year

Most states limit Medigap to ten standard plans ranging from Plan A, the basic plan, to Plan J which is the most comprehensive. In deciding whether to enrol in Medigap, the elderly should:

- Not buy more policies than needed
- Be careful when replacing an existing policy
- Not be pressurized
- Know the company involved
- Check the right to renew
- Look for exclusions
- Decide on the date when it becomes effective

Morris H had always enjoyed good health. Then, at the age of ninety-two, he had a major stroke. Immediately he was hospitalized and he had the full range of medical care including extensive physical and speech therapy. He made a very good recovery, but six months later the doctors discovered that pressure was building up in his brain. If he was not to die, he needed a difficult and risky operation on his skull. Again he survived this and was eventually allowed to return home. However there was considerable brain damage as a result of the surgery and he was never again his lively, irascible self.

His wife was very worried about possible medical bills. He had

had a great deal of highly skilled treatment. However, everything, except for one ambulance ride, was paid for by a combination of Medicare and a subsidiary insurance policy.

Medicaid

Medicaid is a government health insurance for those on low-income. Unlike Medicare which is regulated by the federal government, Medicaid is a joint federal and state programme. The federal government sets guidelines and then states establish their own rules. Those who qualify are eligible to receive both Medicare and Medicaid. Medicaid covers most health costs, including nursing-home care and some skilled home assistance. Some doctors and nursing homes will not take patients on Medicaid or will accept only a limited number. The following are covered:

- Inpatient and outpatient hospital services
- Physician services
- Periodic tests
- Laboratory services
- Rural health clinics
- Nursing home care
- Home health care
- Medical transportation

Some programmes also include:

- Prescription drugs
- Prosthetic devices
- Eye care
- Transportation
- Rehabilitation
- Home care
- Dental Care

The National Health Service

Hospital care
The situation in Great Britain is completely different. When the National Health Service was set up in 1948, it was promised that all British citizens would be looked after 'from the cradle to the grave'. Everyone is expected to register with a General Practitioner. He or she will refer the ill person to a specialist or to a hospital if it is necessary. All specialists, hospital care, prescribed medicines and physical and psychiatric therapy is free.

Side by side with this comprehensive system is a network of private hospitals. Again you must be referred by your General Practitioner. These hospitals provide private rooms and, sometimes, speedier treatment. It is possible to take out private health insurance to cover the cost.

Nursing home care
Nursing home care is not provided by the National Health Service unless the patient has a capital (including the cost of their home) of less than approximately £16,000 ($28,000). If the old person has more money than that, he or she must pay the cost of nursing home care until the capital is spent. It is possible to insure for future nursing home care, although there is no certainty that the elderly person will ever need it.

Care at home
If the family are willing to care for the old person at home various state benefits are payable including a small care allowance for the old person and a carer's allowance for the carer. These benefits are not means-tested and are available for everyone.

> After Muriel P fell and broke her hip, she was taken to hospital. There her hip was pinned and she was given a full course of physiotherapy. Her hospital stay lasted three weeks, including a week in the hospital's convalescent section. Then the hospital

wanted to discharge her. Muriel's children were all in full-time jobs. There was no one to take care of her, so a place was found for her in a private nursing home. Muriel was very unhappy. She felt it was inordinately expensive and she longed to return to her apartment. When she did go back, she was visited twice by her general practitioner; the social services provided various physical aides such as a raised toilet seat and crutches and she was visited three times by a physiotherapist. All these visits and services were free. Then, with the agreement of the GP, Muriel's daughter applied for a care allowance for her mother. Muriel was delighted with the money and she was persuaded to employ a woman several times a week to give her a bath and to prepare a few meals. Because of these arrangements Muriel could continue to live in her own home for several more years.

7

Residential homes and assisted living

For many elderly people, living at home can become too much of a responsibility. In such cases a residential home may be the best solution. Here elderly people live under one roof, spending much of their time in communal sitting and dining rooms. All residents normally have their own bedroom, although in some facilities they may be expected to share accommodation. They receive most of their meals in a common dining room. There are also staff employed by the home to help with washing, dressing, feeding, getting in and out of bed, and using the lavatory.

More luxurious alternatives exist, particularly in the US. Here the facility looks like a giant apartment block. Residents have their own independent flats, but the rent includes cleaning and a certain number of meals (generally thirty) every month in the communal dining room. The management also provides a range of activities and transportation, and employs a number of aides to assist the old people if they need help bathing or dressing.

Yet another alternative is known as assisted living. Residents live in their own studio apartments, but the rent includes all meals and extensive assistance by staff with personal care. Here the care is not dissimilar from that of a nursing home.

> Martha W. and her husband Ned lived in their own home. They were both in their late eighties. Ned had had one stroke, but had made a good recovery. Martha was slowly going blind through cataracts and macular degeneration. Although someone came in twice a week to clean and a lawyer friend of the family had taken charge of their financial affairs, they were largely on their own. Their only child, a son, was in his fifties and lived with his wife in a distant city.
>
> It was becoming clear that Martha and Ned were not really coping. The lawyer summoned the son to discuss the situation. The son had never been very close to his parents; they had lived far away from each other since he had gone to college at the age of seventeen. In any event the old people did not want to move from their neighbourhood. They had lived there for many years and they still had friends. It was decided that they would move into an apartment in the nearby residential facility. This was a huge apartment block; there were more than a hundred units and there was an assisted living wing attached. Their house was sold and they managed to obtain a flat on the seventh floor with a balcony and a beautiful view, which Ned greatly enjoyed. Sadly Martha could no longer see it, but she liked to know it was there. It took them a little time to settle in, but at the end of six months they had made friends and greatly enjoyed many of the activities on offer.
>
> One of the most excellent benefits of the new arrangement was the sense of security it gave them both. If one of them grew more infirm, he or she could always be moved into the assisted living wing and they would still be under one roof. There would be no question of separation unless one of them needed full-time nursing care.

Basic requirements

For those who decide to move into a residential home, there are a number of basic requirements:

- privacy
- comfort
- warmth
- suitable food
- sympathetic staff
- clean clothing
- toilet training and incontinence pads and pants
- help with bathing and washing
- hand rails along walls
- care when sick
- a good sized bedroom with furniture including a bed, chair, wardrobe, chest of drawers, curtains, bed linen, towels, and hand basin or separate bathroom
- clean and comfortable communal areas
- a welcoming and quiet place to receive visitors

For residents with special needs, other requirements should be provided:

Residents who are blind need:
- staff who can guide them to the bathroom
- a clear pathway from their chair to the door of their room
- literature for the blind as well as talking books
- a trained guide dog if possible

For residents who suffer from deafness:
- a loop system
- staff who are able to use sign language

In addition all residents will benefit from:

- suitable activities such as table tennis, board games, and wheelchair games
- adequate space
- planned activities such as concerts and lectures
- occasional outings

Once Cynthia P. was ninety, it was clear that the time had come to move into a residential home. Cynthia was very reluctant to lose her independence and was determined to remain in the same city. Her daughters set themselves the task of finding somewhere suitable. It was not easy. Cynthia lived in a desirable area in a big city; real estate was not cheap and residential homes were few. Basically there were two in the neighbourhood. Both were phenomenally expensive and they were both run by private health care companies.

The daughters were horrified. The first had an indefinable, but unpleasant smell. Very few staff seemed to be around. The communal areas looked desolate. At eleven o'clock, yesterday's newspapers had still not been cleared away; the chairs had not been straightened and the carpet was littered with crumbs. The bedrooms were tiny and the old people were sitting around with little to occupy them. There were two rooms vacant. The paintwork was filthy, but the administrator seemed keen that Cynthia should move in within the week.

The second was a little better. At least it appeared clean and there seemed to be plenty of staff. However they had great difficulty finding anyone who could speak English and when the supervisor finally emerged out of his office, the rooms turned out to be even smaller than in the previous home. The daughters knew that Cynthia would be miserable confined in such a space.

They realized that they would have to extend their search. Eventually they found a very nice home in a nearby suburb. It had started life as an elegant manor house and a purpose-built extension had been added. They stayed for lunch and the food was excellent. The staff seemed nice; the old people were lively and the rooms were a reasonable size. Best of all, Cynthia was allowed to bring her cat. Although she was initially reluctant, in the event, Cynthia settled down quicker than he did (he had some trouble with the existing residential cat!), but over all it turned out to be an excellent choice for them both.

Assessing needs

Before choosing a residential home, it is important to assess an elderly individual's needs. Initially, one should make the same list of personal details as would be necessary for hospital care. All the same information will be needed by a residential home. It should include:

- Full name and date of birth
- Current address and telephone number
- Next of kin
- Past and current illness
- Current medications
- Whether the person is mobile
- If they suffer from any pain
- Name of doctor as well as address and phone number
- Hospital appointments
- Past employment

In making an assessment of needs, you should try to establish how the elderly cope with daily living. Do they have help from social services or home care? Is the person incapacitated? Can they make their own meals, take food and drink to the table, sit down, eat and drink without help? Do they suffer from any illness that requires a special diet? Can they get to and from the lavatory? Do they suffer from incontinence? Are they in pain? Do they have difficulty breathing? Is there a problem with speech, hearing or sight? Is there any sign of dementia?

Different types of care homes

There are different kinds of buildings that can be converted into residential homes. Purpose built properties have been specially built to cater for the elderly. Alternatively, older properties are sometimes converted for the elderly who need residential care. Some of these converted buildings were manor houses or parts of a country estate with beautiful gardens. The corridors may be less convenient than in a purpose built facility with steps and awkward corners. However the rooms tend to be spacious with high ceilings. In general the ratio of staff to residents is lower than in a nursing home because less personal care is needed. When selecting a residential home, it is important to study the brochures provided. You should bear in mind that photographs can be misleading. Brochures offer only limited information, and they may be out of date. They are also often produced by clever public relations firms. Nonetheless those that have instant appeal should be selected first. You should write down what is most attractive and assess if the facilities provided meet the particular elderly person's requirements. The residential home should also be in the right area so the elderly person can keep in touch with old friends.

The next step should be to make an appointment to view the home. Be sure to note how a phone call is dealt with. Is the person who answered polite and encouraging? It is sensible to visit each residential home separately rather than seeing several on the same day. When visiting the home, be sure to ask any relevant questions. This is not a time to be embarrassed. After all, it is your parents' comfort and care which is being discussed. All vital issues should be explored. It is best to make a list beforehand and it is also only fair to tell the truth about the old person in question. If he or she is very difficult or cantankerous, the facility should have some warning. It is vital to establish a good and honest relationship with the staff from the outset.

Melinda J. was not going to be an easy candidate for an old peoples' home. She had been an only child of elderly parents and the whole house had revolved around her. She had never been away to school or college; she was too precious and her parents kept her at home. When she married in her mid-twenties, she chose a man nearly twenty years older than herself who carried on where her parents had left off. He adored her and, even when three children appeared, the entire household centred round her needs and desires.

The two daughters married young. They were anxious to get away from their mother's domination, particularly after their father died. The son was never allowed to marry. There had been occasional girl-friends, but Melinda had perfected a technique for seeing them off. The reality was she was very charming. When she was in a good mood, she was enormous fun and her son, who had always been spoiled, was totally dependent on her emotionally.

Yet once she was over ninety, the situation became impossible. She could not manage day-to-day living. She was becoming malnourished and her apartment was filthy. Her daughters took a deep breath and started looking for an old people's home. It was a long search. They knew their mother would be miserable and would sulk if she was not the centre of attention. Eventually they realized what was needed. They saw that if she went to an assisted living facility before she really needed it, she would be the most able-bodied person there. She could find a role helping the other old people, wheeling them about and talking to them when the staff were busy. Although she continued to complain and was forever telling her daughters how unhappy and neglected she felt, in fact she became invaluable. The supervisor, who only saw her at her delightful best, used to make a point of coming out of her office to tell the daughters whenever they visited how wonderful their mother was!

The size of the home is an important consideration. Some people enjoy being in a home with a large number of residents. Others prefer a smaller facility. Larger residential homes have fifty beds or more. In such cases, there may be two or three floors depending on the number of residents. With multiple levels a lift must be provided to take residents to their own floor. Access is also provided by stairways. In some homes, the floors are complete with a small kitchen, lounge and dining area as well as bathrooms, toilets, and a nurses' station. Smaller nursing homes are often designed in a single storey building. Normally the space is divided into wings with bathrooms, a linen cupboard, storage space, a lounge and dining room. In some cases, they are arranged around an enclosed garden.

Room sizes in residential homes vary. The modern trend is to have single rooms for individuals and double rooms for married couples. When making inspections of care facilities, you should take into consideration:

- room size
- decor
- windows
- door sizes
- furniture
- safety factors
- general suitability

Not all residential homes have en suite bathrooms. Some have rooms with their own bathroom facilities; others only have a toilet. Generally rooms are provided with a hand basin and hot and cold water. En suite facilities are sometimes too small to be of use to a disabled person. In such cases, it is better for the elderly to use larger communal bathrooms and toilets. As far as laundry is concerned, almost all homes have an in-house laundry where residents' clothing is washed and ironed. It is taken from the person's room and returned. Laundry services generally do not include articles that need dry cleaning. Doctors may be willing to continue to visit patients in a residential home to monitor their progress, give advice, and prescribe drugs. However, if it is not practical for visits to take place, there must be enough staff for residents to be taken to see their doctor. Alternatively, the home may insist that the new resident registers with the home's doctor.

Many residential establishments have a leisure programme. These include activities such as craft-work, storytelling, games, bingo, cards, music and movement, board games, fitness classes, film shows, making items for special functions, and knitting and sewing. Some care establishments have a minibus to take residents on outings. On some occasions there may be a solo musician or a group who entertain residents. Generally there is a library. In addition, it is usual to have a shop or trolley with writing paper, envelopes, stamps and other items for the old people to buy. Many residential homes have gardens. This is a very desirable facility. Old people enjoy going out on a fine day to sit in the fresh air. At holiday time it is usual for residential homes to organize festivities.

Visitors are normally encouraged to participate in the life of the residential home. Keeping in touch with the outside world and with old friends and family is important. Therefore a good residential home will have plenty of car-parking space for visitors and visitors will be encouraged to have coffee and to stay for meals. This, of course, gives the visitor a chance to check up on the standard of catering and whether their parent is being properly nourished. Most important of all, the atmosphere should be such that friends and family should feel welcome and the staff should be accessible so that questions can be asked if there are any concerns.

> Lisa G. was Jewish. Although she was not Orthodox and did not need a special diet, she had always been strict with her children and prevented them from celebrating Christian festivals or having a Christmas tree. Therefore, when she went into a residential home, Lisa's son was rather nervous. He discovered that both Christmas and Easter were celebrated. There was a Christmas tree; local schoolchildren came in to sing carols and everyone had little presents and a large Christmas dinner. A similar pattern was repeated at Easter with everyone enjoying Easter eggs. However it was an excellent home in every other respect so the son waited to see how Lisa would react.

In the event she loved it. She had always been artistic and she participated in helping to decorate the Christmas tree. She enjoyed choosing Christmas presents for all her friends and was like a child on Christmas morning when she opened her own parcels. Later, when Easter came around, she found more Easter eggs than anyone else in the Easter Egg Hunt. When her son expressed surprise at her attitude, Lisa said very severely, 'There's nothing wrong in helping other people celebrate their religion!'

Choosing a residential home

There are many considerations when choosing a residential home. The following should serve as a check list, to be gone through systematically:

- access to rooms
- activities
- bath hoists
- bathrooms
- bedrooms
- commode
- dining room
- furniture
- gardens
- insurance certificate
- kitchens
- lifts
- lounge
- meal times
- menus
- pets
- position of toilets
- post
- quiet room

- registration certificate
- smokers' room
- staffing levels
- wheelchair ramps

You might want to ask these questions:

- Can an elderly person have a single room?
- Is a diabetic diet provided?
- Are incontinence pads available?
- Is a laundry located on site?
- Is there transportation to places of worship or for shopping?
- Are there provisions for religious services in the residential home?
- What are visiting hours?
- Does a doctor visit the home?
- How can one make a complaint?
- Are there fire drills?
- What happens if someone needs to go to hospital?
- Are residents taken out by the staff?
- Does the residential home have functions at festival time?
- Does anyone help with taking medicine?

When visiting a residential home, you should also use your senses:

Smell
- Does the home smell clean?
- Is there an odour of urine?
- Is there a smell of body odour?
- Are there smells of stale food or cooking?

Touch
- Are chairs clean and dry?
- Is furniture polished?

Sight
- Do the residents look clean?
- Do they look happy?
- Are the staff uniforms clean?

Hearing
- Do you hear people talking in a friendly fashion?
- Do residents talk to each other?
- Is the television on too loudly?

Taste
- Is food fresh?

In assessing a residential home, you should look at rules such as:

- keeping fire doors closed
- keeping existing doors free from obstruction
- medications being locked up
- hoists being used for residents
- residents being barred from certain areas

Residential homes also have inspections and certificates. You should look to see if:

- premises are safe and clean
- residents are comfortable
- kitchens and food stored safely
- menus are balanced
- drugs are properly stored
- care of residents is done properly

Finances

Unless the elderly person has very little capital, a residential home is a serious financial commitment. When visiting residential homes, you will need to compare costs. Before you make a visit, you should make a list of questions:

- Are monthly accounts sent out?
- Are there extra charges?
- When are fees due?
- Can fees be paid by direct debit?
- Do social services send contributions to the residential home?

In making a financial assessment, you should list all the old person's income:

- state pension
- private pension
- disability allowances
- annuity income
- investment income
- savings
- stocks and shares
- rented property

Frequently the residential home's fees are listed in the brochure. This normally includes:

- care
- resident's room
- bed linen
- towels
- meals
- laundry
- light and heating

Other costs may include:

- double rooms used as a single room
- en suite bathroom
- refreshments and meals for visitors
- incontinence aids
- hiring of special equipment
- extra staff
- dry cleaning
- occupational therapy
- hairdressing
- outings
- speech therapy
- chiropody
- doctor's visits
- prescriptions
- shopping

Making a second visit

Do not trust your first impression. The home may be having an unusually good day. Make a arrangements to visit a second time. This is the opportunity to:

- Introduce the relative to the matron or nurse
- Ask if they can be shown bedrooms, communal rooms and other parts of the home
- Encourage the elderly person to speak to staff members
- Allow the elderly person to ask questions
- Ask to see the menus
- Ask the matron or nurse to discuss the daily routine

Matty A. lived on her own. She had been a widow for many years and her only child, a son, was a very busy journalist. When it became clear that she needed a residential home, the son said he would organize it. In fact he decided on the first one he visited. The supervisor was very pleasant. She said that her daughter wanted to be a journalist and they had a good chat about the child's prospects. The home itself looked basic and institutional, but it was in a convenient location and it was a reasonable price. In any case the son was under a lot of pressure at work and he really did not have time to make a series of visits.

When Matty moved in, the whole thing was a disaster. She was given a poky little room overlooking an inner courtyard. She was a lifelong vegetarian, but there was no provision for vegetarian diets and when she asked, most of the kitchen staff did not speak English. Eventually when she did explain to someone why she could not eat lunch, she was given to understand that she must just adapt to the home's ways. Within a week all her jewellery had disappeared; there was nothing of great monetary worth, but it had enormous sentimental value. Also the staff were overworked and they were not gentle. Matty had to have help dressing in the morning. She was pushed about and a large bruise appeared on her arm.

It was two weeks before her son came to visit. He told himself that his mother needed time to settle in. When he did come, he was horrified to find how thin she had grown. She was very tearful and she clung to him desperately when it was time for him to go. It was clear that this experiment was not working.

Moving in

When making a transition to residential accommodation, elderly people may mourn the loss of:

- their home
- their independence
- seeing friends

- previous carers
- neighbours
- possessions
- pets

Relatives who have been carers may also feel guilty about the move. They may feel they have let down their mother, father, aunt or uncle. They may find it difficult to believe that their relative needs specialist care. While it is natural to feel this way, you should accept that what residential homes offer to residents is a full range of facilities as well as new opportunities. To ease the transition, you should:

- Explain the situation to family members and friends and encourage them to visit
- Give visitors the new address
- Making out a visiting rota
- Ask the staff to encourage relatives to make new friends

It will take time for the elderly person to settle in, (maybe as much as six months) but a residential home has many advantages, providing a friendly, comfortable and secure place to live where adequate care is constantly available. Inevitably, those who go to residential homes will feel stress. Before admission, you should:

- Talk to your relative in a positive way
- Emphasize the disadvantages of remaining at home
- Take them to see the home
- Point out the advantages of moving to a home
- Encourage relatives to ask questions when visiting the home
- Discuss every step
- Keep them informed
- Encourage them to help prepare for the move
- Arrange a trial period if possible
- Indicate that they will be able to take some possessions with them

Gerald P really did not want to go into a residential home. He had never married; he was very competent domestically and he loved his apartment. However, it was clear to his niece, who was his closest relation, that he was slowly becoming more confused and frail. Everything was more of a struggle and she persuaded her uncle to go and look at the alternatives. They visited several residential homes and he did not like any of them. Then the niece made another suggestion. What about some form of sheltered housing? Near the city in which Gerald had lived all his life, there was being built a 'Continuing Care' retirement community. The idea was that old people could live independently for as long as possible. The community provided aides who could come into their apartments to help them if it was necessary. There was also a restaurant where they could eat meals if they did not feel up to cooking and there was a small shop for basic supplies. Then, when Gerald needed more help, he could graduate to a residential home in which all his meals were provided and there was also a nursing home in the complex if he became completely incapacitated.

Gerald was attracted to this idea. As a single man, he knew the importance of friends and he knew how difficult it was to meet new people at his age. In this community, he would have the opportunity of getting to know some new faces while he was still moderately independent. He could bring in his own furniture and he would not feel that he was on the scrap-heap.

He adapted very well to his new life. Sadly within a year, he had a major heart-attack, but because there was a fully-equipped nursing home in the community, there was somewhere for him to go when he left hospital where he was properly looked after. Altogether the niece felt that they had both made a very good choice.

Continuing care retirement communities

At present, these facilities are only commonly found in the US. They offer accommodation ranging from completely independent living for the over fifties to nursing home care. Many will accept only those who are mobile and can live independently initially. Once a resident is admitted, care is offered for the duration of the person's life. The centres normally include apartments for those who are able to live independently and offer activities including golf, swimming, tennis, lectures, films and outings. They also have an assisted-living complex, which provides care and services for those who need help with daily tasks such as bathing, dressing, and eating. There is also a nursing home attached to the complex for residents who are frail or ill. While such residences are expensive, they offer companionship and care. Entrance fees vary greatly, ranging from $20,000 (£12,000) to $400,000 (£240,000). This fee may include the cost of a house or apartment. In some cases, part of the entrance fee is returned to the resident's estate when the person dies or moves. There are also monthly fees. Generally residents choose from three types of arrangement:

1. Extended or all-inclusive contracts that cover all costs. The entry fee and monthly fees cover all health care including unlimited nursing care.
2. Modified contracts that cover only a limited number of days of nursing care.
3. Fee-for-service contracts which provide residents with independent living and assisted living services, but require the full cost of nursing care.

It is very important that the elderly person becomes part of the community when still young enough to establish themselves and to make friends. There also may be a problem if circumstances change – for example if children have to move to the other end of the country. Enquiries must be made in advance about what happens if the old person wants to move out. However, if it can be afforded, this option is the ideal solution for many people.

8

Finding a nursing home

A T SOME POINT an elderly person may find that nursing home care is a necessity. Making the decision to take such a step can be overwhelming. There is no disguising that this is the last phase. The end is coming and death is not far away. Even if the elderly suffer from illness or chronic pain, such a transition can be devastating. In order to minimise the inevitable sense of loss and desolation that can arise, it is important to prepare as much as possible. The worst possible situation is one in which the elderly person needs a nursing home urgently; everyone scurries around; only one vacancy can be found at such short notice. It is not in a convenient location and it does not really offer the type of care the old person needs, but, as the old proverb has it, beggars can't be choosers.

Deborah P. and Judith B. were sisters. Both were widows and they lived in the same town. Deborah's heart was weak and when she became immobile it was clear she needed to be in a nursing home. No one had made any preparations. Her children lived far away and eventually the doctor found a place in a nursing home the other side of town. It was not a very nice place. The staff were overworked. Deborah was dependant on a bell, often she rang and rang, but no one came to her. Deborah was miserable, but there was little anyone could do. She refused to eat and became weaker. Eventually she was taken to hospital and she was dead within three months.

Judith was ten years younger than her sister. She was appalled at what had happened to Deborah. She started making enquiries and she insisted that her children, when they came to visit, took her on little expeditions to see the various nursing home options. Finally she picked one she liked. It was out in the country, had a beautiful garden and, most importantly, was willing to take Alzheimer patients. Judith and Deborah's mother had had Alzheimer's disease and Judith had always been afraid that one day it might happen to her. She kept in touch with the home, paid a deposit and put her name on a waiting list.

A few years later she realized she was becoming more forgetful. This was the moment. She let the nursing home know that she was interested in taking the first room that became available. Within six weeks she had moved and she spent two very happy years there. The care was excellent and, although she died of a stroke before her short-term memory completely disappeared, her children were very thankful for the expertise and kindness Judith experienced.

Deciding to move

The thought of a nursing home may conjure up images of old people forced to live in cramped and unpleasant conditions. But such a conception gives a distorted picture of contemporary nursing home care. Most nursing homes have adequate staff, improved staff training, as well as ample activities to keep residents occupied. Today it is possible for residents to receive good medical and personal care. Nursing homes offer facilities beyond what is available in the home or in a residential facility. Yet, it is not uncommon for those who are responsible for their relatives' care to feel uneasy about making this decision. Reactions to putting an elderly person in a home include:

- Guilt that one has not done enough
- Anxiety that the nursing staff will not do enough
- Anxiety over the high cost of nursing care
- Guilt that one doesn't visit enough
- Anxiety for having to visit often
- Guilt for feeling relief that a relative is in a nursing home
- Anxiety that the nursing home will not be adequate and that another plan will have to be formulated
- Guilt about promising in the past that a nursing home would not be necessary

It can be seen from the above catalogue that nursing homes arouse a confused array of emotions.

Angus A was a widower. He was diabetic and he suffered from bad angina. He was looked after devotedly by his daughter. She was married with children and also held down a full-time job, but she still visited her father twice every day, preparing his meals and helping him wash and dress.

Her health began to suffer. Her husband and children felt they were being neglected; her employer told her that she was too preoccupied with her domestic responsibilities. Then Angus fell in the bathroom. His daughter did not have the strength to get him up and an ambulance had to be called. It was clear that something had to be done. Both her husband and the doctor urged her to consider a nursing home. Initially she would not countenance the idea, but, when Angus fell a second time, the move became inevitable.

The daughter was wracked with guilt, particularly as it took Angus a little time to settle in. In fact it was the only possible solution. The family could relax at home. The employer was satisfied. Angus could be visited every day and was being properly looked after. Nonetheless the guilt did not go away and she always wished it had been possible to care for her father at home.

Despite such concerns, care at home can often be inadequate. Sometimes caregivers are unable to function successfully. It is even possible for family members to be neglectful or abusive. Sometimes the care is so intensive that the caregiver suffers stress and ends up needing care themselves. Most nursing homes offer basic medical care and constant nursing. Meals are provided as well as laundry services, personal care, counselling, recreation, social services, rehabilitative programmes, as well as a pharmacy. Some contain special wings or floors that provide hospital care. Generally nursing homes are required for relatively brief periods while a person recuperates, or alternatively for longer periods of time if the old person is chronically or terminally ill. Nursing homes are privately owned, publicly supported or run by a religious or civic group.

Looking for a nursing home

When you begin a search for a nursing home, location will be a paramount factor. Should elderly persons be moved near their children, or should a nursing home be near where they currently live? There are a number of issues to consider:

- **Certificate and licensing**. Nursing homes should be certified by the authorities. Certification ensures that the home meets established standards, has passed an inspection, and is regularly monitored
- **Intuition**. It is generally advisable to follow one's initial instincts about a nursing home. You should consider what deterred you. What surprises were found? Don't be influenced by interior decorating or gardens. Walk through the entire complex to ascertain the conditions of the various

facilities. Observe how residents are cared for

- **Cleanliness and maintenance.** A nursing home should smell fresh. It should be well maintained in the lobby and public rooms as well as in the residents' facilities. You should check whether the furnishings are in good repair. Is there plaster cracking from the walls for example?
- **Safe.** Is there ample security? Are pathways clear? Are there ladders at the windows? Are there grab bars in the hall? Is the neighbourhood safe?
- **Staffing levels.** Nursing homes should have at least one staff member for every five residents during the day: these are registered nurses, licensed practical nurses, or certified nursing assistants. The ratio in the evening can be at least one to ten, or at night one to fifteen. In special wings, the ratio should be higher. Many nursing homes do not reach this target
- **Homeliness.** Nursing homes should be comfortable. The lounge sought to be inviting and rooms adequate. It is important to ascertain if residents are allowed to bring their own furniture. Are the old people treated as individuals? Is there privacy as well as a degree of community living? Can residents have pets?
- **Caring staff.** It is vitally important that the staff are pleasant and helpful. They should have good relations with residents. It is important that they are encouraging and supportive
- **Residents.** It is crucial that a visit is made to the nursing home. Are residents well-cared for? Do they look content? Are they restrained in chairs, beds, and wheelchairs? Do they participate in activities or sit in their rooms? Do they have friendships? Are they happy with the care they receive?
- **Daily activity.** You should check to see if independence is encouraged. Do residents get fresh air and exercise? Is there a range of activities? Is their a place for exercise, or a pool?
- **Availability.** Is there a waiting list? If so, what is the approximate length of time? Is it possible for someone to be cared for at home prior to admission?

- **Medical Care.** Are nurses available at all times? Are doctors on the staff? Is the nursing home close to a hospital?
- **Food.** When you go to visit the nursing home, ask if you can have a meal. What is the food like? Is it nutritious? Can the kitchen accommodate special needs?
- **Director.** When you visit, ask to see the Director. You should attempt to ascertain the policies of the nursing home and whether it is a suitable place.
- **Resident Council.** You should ask if there is a resident council. How often does it meet? What issues does it discuss? Is the nursing home responsive to suggestions?
- **Room Change.** It is important to check if room changes are permitted, and if so, are there any extra costs? Find out if the nursing home has a policy about moving residents to other rooms. What happens if a resident is hospitalized – will the person's room be retained? Under what circumstances could a resident be discharged?
- **Religion.** Does the nursing home cater to all religions? Are there religious services?
- **Hospice.** Does the nursing home provide hospice care?

Myrtle went to a nursing home after she became too lame and confused to be cared for at home. Her children had taken a lot of trouble to choose a good establishment, and in general they were very satisfied with their mother's care. However, it was clear that Myrtle was becoming increasingly depressed. She complained that everything was so dark. Initially the children wondered if her spectacles needed changing, but her optician said there was nothing wrong with them.

Then one of the nurses pointed out that Myrtle's room faced north. She never got any sunlight. The situation was discussed and it was agreed that as soon as a south-facing room became available, she would move. Myrtle was lucky. Her new room was available within a month and it was amazing how quickly she perked up. She had always loved sitting in the sun and it was clearly a necessity for her.

Admission to a nursing home

Once a nursing home has been chosen, the admission process will begin. A variety of forms including the elderly person's medical, financial and legal records will need to be supplied. Some nursing homes demand a deposit before admission. You should check to see whether this will be refunded if the resident leaves early. If the elderly person's care is to be covered by Medicare or Medicaid (in the US) or by the National Health Service (in the UK), a deposit cannot be required. A nursing home contract should include information about costs, payment schedules, services provided, penalties for failure to pay, and the home's refund policy as well as bed holding policy if hospitalization is necessary. It is advisable to have the document checked by a lawyer. You should check for clauses that free a home from liability for injury or loss of possessions.

Moving to a nursing home

The act of moving to a nursing home is traumatic for all those involved. An elderly person may be nervous, depressed, and frightened. These feelings are natural, and should be recognized. The person moving in is facing a major transition. It is important that everyone remains calm. It is vital not to make a change of plan. There are several steps that should be undertaken in advance:

- In the weeks before the move, it is important to bring the elderly person to visit the home several times
- Ask friends and family to be supportive of this decision. They might want to come visit the home themselves and talk with the elderly person before the move
- Hold a party for the elderly person before the move. Guests should bring gifts for the person to take to the nursing home such as framed photos, silk flowers, a bathrobe, slippers, a scarf, scent, or potpourri

- It is important that there should be pictures on the wall of the new room. This might be a chance for a selection of grandchildren's photographs
- Before packing the car, find out exactly what the elderly person is allowed to bring. If furniture is permitted, this should be sent in advance
- Get others to help. They can arrange the room at the nursing home and have a meal with the elderly person on arrival. It is important that the old person feels that there is continuity with his or her past life
- If the elderly person has a fixed routine, ask the staff to make suitable arrangements if at all possible

Rosa P.'s daughter took a lot of trouble to make sure her mother's room in the nursing home was as comfortable and homely as possible. Rosa herself was in the last stages of dementia and many of the family felt that the daughter's concern was pointless. In any event, Rosa did not relax. She fretted and was clearly unhappy. Then her grand-daughter had an inspiration. Rosa loved flowers and her house always smelt of gardenias or lily-of-the-valley. Although her daughter had made sure that she had a supply of fresh flowers, it was not enough. So the grand-daughter went out and bought an array of room-scents. Once the room was sprayed regularly with lily-of-the-valley, Rosa settled down and seemed content.

Assessment

When a person is admitted to a nursing home, there must be a full assessment of their condition. This will involve a review of the person's physical, functional, social, and mental condition. Staff will examine the overall health of the individual including hearing and vision and ability to perform daily tasks. The staff should also take note of any habits, hobbies and relationships. This assessment normally takes place within fourteen days of a resident's admission.

The staff will put together a plan of care that lists medical treatments, describes therapy and nursing care, and recommends activities that should be followed or avoided. This plan should be devised by a team of nurses, dieticians, social workers, and members of the activity staff. Ideally family members should be also be involved.

Visiting the nursing home

Visiting the nursing home can be stressful. But, you should bear in mind that even if the visit is brief, or if the resident complains the entire time, or even if the person forgets that the visit has occurred, it is important to make the effort. It communicates to the staff that you care about the person and it also provides an opportunity to observe the standard of care which is offered. In fact you should visit as often as possible. Be sure to consult with staff members. There are a number of things that should be done while visiting:

- Don't routinely schedule visits – it is better to drop by unexpectedly so that everyday care can be monitored
- By law relatives can visit whenever they wish. Be sure to visit at times when you can carefully observe how staff deal with residents. Be respectful of any reasons that might limit visiting hours, but don't be put off visiting when you feel it is most suitable
- Plan visits around the resident's schedule
- Visits can be short; residents can tire easily
- If visits are uncomfortable, do something active. Playcards; take residents to lunch; help with writing a letter; read mail or a newspaper; look through a photo album; encourage the resident to reminisce about the past
- Pamper the resident. Help the elderly person with personal tasks, such as a manicure, a foot message, putting on makeup or arranging hair
- Make physical contact with the elderly person. Do not

hesitate to kiss them or hug them if you have that sort of relationship
- Don't feel you have to talk the entire time. Being in the same room is reassuring
- If the resident has difficulty eating, visit during mealtimes and help the person by cutting food and feeding them if necessary
- Bring children to visit
- If you have the flu or a cold, postpone the visit. Old people are vulnerable
- Don't say you will visit unless you are certain that you can go. A cancelled visit can be very disappointing
- Keep the resident informed about what is happening with friends and relatives. Photos and videos are helpful. Don't hide bad news; it is best to be open about what is taking place
- Review the elderly person's clothes. Is there anything that is needed? Ask aides if there is something that should be purchased to make the person more comfortable
- Make contact with staff

Marlene J had always dressed fashionably. She loved clothes and had several full wardrobes in her house. When she became confined to a wheelchair and needed an array of medications for a slow-growing cancer, her children felt she must move into a nursing home. Inevitably the question arose what would she wear. Marlene's daughters were well-aware that the staff would be busy and they purchased a series of easy-care, elastic-wasted, front-fastening garments in pastel colours. Marlene was appalled. In her view those kind of clothes were suitable only for very young children. She insisted on describing them as 'romper-suits' and would have no part in them.

On the other hand her beautiful designer clothes and her elegant high-heeled shoes were not the answer either. In the end, the staff were consulted. There was no doubt that they preferred the 'romper-suits'. The daughters realized that even more money needed to be spent. They got in touch with a manufacturer of elegant designer sports clothes and they sat down with their mother. Together they pored over the catalogue and eventually they agreed on a whole new elegant wardrobe of beautiful, comfortable, easy-care separates.

It is important to express concern to staff about any problems. If an elderly person's room mate keeps the person up at night; if you notice change in the person's sleep habits or weight; if the resident will not eat the food in the dining room, you should consult the appropriate staff. You should try to devise solutions, but, at the same time, must try not to overburden the nursing home.

You should also be alert to any signs of neglect including bruises, bedsores, soiled bed sheets, poor hygiene, weight loss, and excessive fear. There have been scandals in nursing homes of abusive staff and general neglect. For every scandal that is uncovered, probably two have never come to light. Therefore it is very important to be vigilant. Even the best-run nursing home may be unfortunate enough to employ one bad member of staff.

> May F. suffered from severe dementia. She could no longer recognize family members and seemed to be in a world of her own. Generally she seemed content in her nursing home. Then, suddenly, her attitude changed. She seemed to shrink as if she were expecting a blow and there was an unexplained bruise on her arm. May's son was not happy about this. He found out who was looking after his mother and went to discuss the matter with the administrator. It turned out that a new aide had recently been employed on May's floor. She came with satisfactory references, but when the supervisor telephoned this woman's previous employed, the referee was hesitant and would not talk about her. The supervisor promised to keep a careful check on the situation. Within a week, this aide was discovered slapping another resident and she was dismissed on the spot.

It is also vital to ensure that the resident is safe. Be alert to any danger of falling. Take note of any ailments that might be overlooked or insufficiently treated, including vision and hearing problems. Be aware of any signs of depression. When there is a concern, try to work together with staff to solve the problem. It is advisable to have one person from the family act as the regular spokesperson. Otherwise the staff may be confused about who is in charge of the resident's care.

Long distance care

If it is not possible to visit the elderly person in a nursing home, try to contact someone who can. Ask relatives or friends or volunteer visitors. Alternatively, you should hire someone who can go to visit regularly and can report back to you. Ask a nurse supervisor how best to be in touch with the staff. Arrange for regular updates. If possible, create a relationship with nurses or aides who see the resident regularly.

It is very easy for an old person to feel isolated and forgotten and it is a sad truth that many old people in nursing homes never have any visitors at all. It is vitally important to keep in contact with the person in the nursing home; use the telephone as often as possible, and send letters and videos. You should talk about your activities, family and the past. If the elderly person can use the internet, communicate by email. You should also send care packages of special food and gifts so that the old person continues to feel cherished. Even if the elderly relative suffers from dementia and appears to have no understanding of the situation, it is still important to keep in touch. There is no doubt that staff in a nursing home pay more attention to those who have regular visitors and who are not forgotten.

> Stanley G. was a widower and Edith J. was a widow. They had been childhood sweethearts and when they found themselves in the same residential home, they wanted to get married. However, there were problems. Because of possible inheritance difficulties (Edith

was very well-off), Edith's children were not keen on the idea. In addition there would have been a substantial loss of social security income. Therefore the two decided to have a little ceremony of blessing from the local minister, but they did not formally get married.

In the course of time, Stanley got ill. He kept having a series of little strokes. He was beginning to need more care than the residential care should offer. Edith had already devotedly looked after one sick husband. She realized that she did not feel the same about Stanley. In addition her children were appalled that their possible inheritance would be spent on Stanley's expensive nursing home. They persuaded their mother that the person who should care for Stanley was his son, a lawyer, who lived on the other side of the country. Stanley was therefore sent off to a nursing home three thousand miles away.

Edith did feel guilty. But legally she had no obligations towards Stanley and she was under considerable pressure from her children. Stanley was no doubt well-cared for in his nursing home, but the son was a busy man and did not have much of a relationship with his father. Stanley's last few months were lonely and sad.

If any difficulties arise about care, you should immediately consult the staff. Talk with the person involved in the first instance. Try to be helpful rather than critical. Be specific about your concerns; explain what has happened. Listen to the staff member and see if it is possible to resolve the problem. If this fails, talk to the staff member's supervisor. If this does not produce results, you should consult the nursing supervisor, medical director or administrator. In all cases you should be calm and respectful. Be careful to document all conversations and make a note of what was said. Keep a record of the time and date. Follow up with phone calls and letters and ask for a written response. If there is no resolution, check if there is a grievance procedure and file a formal complaint.

Evaluating nursing home care

Once an elderly person is in a nursing home, it is important to assess whether the move is working. Is the person more confused? Is the individual complaining more than before? Is there a physical and mental deterioration? It is important to be patient. Normally it takes six months for residents to adjust to a new routine and relationships. There can be setbacks. But most residents do adapt. If the person's complaints are vague, try to find out what is wrong. Is there something that can be done? If you believe the nursing home is the best solution, you should bear in mind:

- Nursing home residents often complain and appear depressed when visitors are around. But when they leave, they return to their activities and friends in good spirits. If there is someone on the staff who has a good relationship with the resident, ask how they are most of the time. You should be aware that you are usually getting a distorted picture of the real situation.
- If the elderly person appears worse every time you visit, it may be that the individual is simply declining. This could be a natural occurrence rather than the fault of the home.
- Adults often project their own emotions on relatives who are in nursing homes. It is important to assess whether the resident is actually unhappy. Possibly you are merely feeling guilty yourself. Never hesitate to ask for a second opinion.

9

Death and funerals

THERE IS ONLY one certainty in life and that is death. Inevitably elderly people will die. This is a difficult and painful realization for all concerned. It is tempting to deny it and pretend that the present situation can go on for ever. In fact it is best to confront the reality. Death is not a single event. It is a process, a final passage, that demands the practical and emotional involvement of the entire family. There is a range of issues that need to be faced as a loved one becomes increasingly frail.

Piers P. had always been very close to his mother. His elder brother was killed in the Second World War and his father died soon afterwards. Piers' mother was a charming, feminine, impractical woman. Piers felt that he was her only protector and he loved the role. For many years they lived happily together in a large apartment. They were a couple; they both loved the theatre and art and they spent many happy hours together on cultural expeditions.

Then, when she was eighty-six, Piers' mother had a stroke. Piers looked after her devotedly at home with the aid of a team of nurses.

No expense was spared and Piers willed her to get better. There was some improvement. Slowly, painfully she learned to speak again and Piers insisted that she was back to her old self. However, a second stroke six months later killed her. Piers was inconsolable. His whole life had been centred around his mother and he found himself, at the age of sixty-one, completely bereft.

Preparation

If there is talk about nothing else, it is necessary to discuss the medical care of the elderly. Hopefully the person has signed advanced directives. Different countries and even different states within the US have different laws about this, but it is generally possible for the elderly person to give clear instructions as to how their end is to be managed. Any form of active euthanasia remains illegal, but in most places it is possible to declare in advance that there should be no resuscitation or artificial aids to prolong survival when there is no realistic hope of recovery.

To avoid the difficulties at this stage, it is essential that steps are taken to help the elderly person:

- Find directives. By now elderly individuals should have signed a living will outlining their wishes regarding medical care at the end of their lives as well as a power of attorney for health care. These documents should be found. Make sure to have a copy; the doctor should also have one. If the elderly person has not signed them, get them signed at once
- Talk about the arrangements. Ideally there should already have been a full discussion about medical care. By this time the doctor should be able to give you some idea of the future, as well as what sorts of decisions need to be faced. Given the person's health and what is known about the future, would the elderly person wish to be put on a respirator? Would the person want artificial nutrition or hydration? Would

resuscitation be advisable? Would the person wish to be resuscitated if the heart were to stop? Would the individual prefer to be at home or under the care of a hospice? It is important to be truthful throughout the discussion. If the elderly person expresses fears, the subject should not be changed – it is better to be honest and comforting

- It may be that decisions have been put off for too long. The elderly person may no longer be able to speak or have a rational opinion. Then these issues must be discussed by the family with the doctor. In any event the attitude of those looking after the old person should always be reassuring and comforting. Even if they cannot communicate, they still need reassurance and company

- People are often more afraid of dying than death; they are frightened by the process, of the unknown, of pain and of being alone. It is a time when an elderly person needs support, assurance, and affection

- The elderly are particularly frightened of pain. Information from the doctor about what is to come and how pain will be controlled should alleviate much of this fear. If the person is not under the care of a hospice, and it is clear they are in pain, you should ask the doctor for a consultation with a palliative care specialist

- Elderly persons are often afraid they will be a burden to their families as they become more ill. They should be reassured they are not a burden, and that their relations will look after them or continue to oversee their care

- It is helpful for the elderly to review their lives, consider what life has meant and think about how they will be remembered. They want to know that their lives have been worthwhile and they have accomplished positive things. You should help the elderly to remember the good things in their lives by talking about happy incidents in the past

- It is important for the elderly to know they will be remembered. You should talk about how the person has helped you and

influenced your life. Let them know their children and
grandchildren will remember them
- The elderly will want to know that their families will be
  provided for and that their affairs are in order. You should
  reassure them that nothing will be left unsettled

Cedric R. was dying of cancer. He was eighty-three. His wife looked
after him devotedly and his three daughters lived nearby and
did what they could. However, Cedric had always had a special
relationship with his son. They were both lawyers and Cedric had
overseen his legal education. Now the son was a very successful
judge in a distant city. The original plan was that the son would take
a week's vacation to come to say goodbye to his father, but, when
he arrived, he realized he must do more. He cancelled his schedule
for three months and announced that he was remaining with his
father.

They sat together every day and the son discussed all his
interesting cases with his father. Cedric could not say much, but it
was clear from his occasional comment that he was following. He
became far calmer and less restive. Strangely, it was a happy time
for the whole household. Cedric could enjoy his family and take
pride in them all. He could particularly enjoy the achievements of
his son, to which he had so greatly contributed. He died within a
month, surrounded by support and love.

Stages of acceptance

Everyone responds in different ways to illness and death. Yet, there
are generally several stages of response:

- **Denial.** Sometimes individuals simply cannot cope with
  distress. Instead of recognizing the realities of illness, there is
  denial. It is important not to force information on the elderly,
  but to allow them to absorb the situation in their own time.

If the person remains in denial and refuses to take proper medication, it is important to inform the doctor or nurse

- **Anger.** When older people recognize the severity of their condition, this can evoke anger at themselves or others. Such emotion can be expressed in fits of rage. If you become the target, try not to respond. Instead, you need to accept that the elderly person is experiencing difficulties and anger is part of the grieving process

- **Bargaining.** Those who are terminally ill often go through a period of bargaining in which they make resolutions to try to avoid the inevitability of their illnesses. This could involve changes in their regime. In such situations, you should accept that this is normal and encourage change if it helps them to feel control over their life

- **Worry and grief.** When individuals realize there is no escape from dying, they may begin to mourn the loss of their life and their loved ones. They may grieve over the things they failed to do in the past and that they had hoped to accomplish. This can cause great sadness and despair. They may also worry about being a burden. You should try to lessen these worries. But you should also try to share in their sadness and grief by listening sympathetically and reassuringly

- **Acceptance.** At some point elderly people become resigned to what is happening. They realize there is nothing they can do to change the situation. If the person has been ill for a considerable time, they may be able to accept their death. Although this can cause considerable sadness, it is best for all concerned. If the person is ready to die, they may wish to see fewer people. If the elderly person refuses to see visitors, this desire should be respected; alternatively, if there is a wish to see certain individuals, this should be arranged if possible

Eleanor I was dying. She had had a stormy life with two divorces. She had never really got on with either of her daughters and she was not enthusiastic about being a grandmother. When it became clear that she was terminally ill, both daughters did their best for her. No one knew how long the final stage would last and everyone, including Eleanor herself, urged the younger daughter to go on a long-planned holiday. During the fortnight she was away, Eleanor took a turn for the worse. She was unconscious much of the time, but she was restless and it was clear she wanted something. Then, the younger daughter returned, brown and fresh from her holiday. As soon as she came into the room, she sat down by the side of the bed with her sister. Eleanor looked at them both, gave a big sigh and died..

Caring for the elderly

At the last stages, there is much that can be done:

- Be aware of the mental and spiritual condition of the person. If he or she is religious, there should be the opportunity to talk to a counsellor or minister
- Make the most of these final days. Think about what the person would appreciate most. Does he or she like music? Is it better to have silence? Would the person prefer to watch television or listen to the radio? Would the person like to reminisce about the past? Would he or she like to look out the window at birds feeding? Is it better to sit by a waterfront? Or would the person simply like to lie in bed and have someone sit alongside?
- Give the person a great deal of affection. Hold the person's hand, stroke her forehead, kiss her cheek, or give her a massage
- Even if the person is unable to express herself, or is oblivious of what is happening, assume that she is able to understand what is going on around her. Don't talk about the person as if she is not there. Talk to her, bathe her, and feed her
- If the person is bedridden, watch for bedsores
- Make sure the room smells fresh

• As the person becomes more ill, consider your own emotional needs. You will need support too

Care at home

If the family feels it is better to have the person at home, you must provide comfort and reassurance. The individual will be surrounded by family members. At home you will be able to create a supportive and caring environment. It is important to keep track of medications as well as be careful to lift and shift the person to prevent bedsores. Even if health aides and nurses are employed to help with such physical activity, home care can be exhausting. You will need to consider whether you have the energy and strength to cope. It might be helpful to phone a hospice to ask for advice how best to deal with the situation. Many hospices are willing to give some basic training in caring for the dying at home.

Hospice

Hospice care – the philosophy and practice of caring for those who are approaching death – is based on the belief that death is a natural part of life. With the help of a hospice, a person who is incurably ill and close to death is removed from the hospital and brought to a comfortable place where they are able to die peacefully. Hospice nurses and doctors do not cure patients; they are there to relieve pain, to provide what is called palliative care. Most hospices will arrange for invasive medical procedures if these will ease pain or treat secondary illnesses. Nurses are trained to manage pain, and they are also able to comfort both patients and their families. They help them through the daily regime and discuss the dying process. They also help to resolve conflicts and provide financial guidance and pastoral support. Almost all hospice services are covered by Medicare and other insurance.

There are many advantages to hospice care, not least the fact that they are experts in pain relief. Unlike an ordinary hospital, the nurses should have time to be with the patients and to talk with them. There are often teams of trained volunteers and the relatives will get more support than in an ordinary hospital. However, admission to a hospice is an acknowledgment that the end is near. Some patients may find this difficult, though for some it may even be a relief.

Barbara P. was a writer. Her novels were small-scale and domestic and she loved the jokes and human peculiarities that make up everyday life. When she was diagnosed with terminal cancer, she was initially cared for at home by her sister, but, ever practical, she decided to go into a hospice for her final days. When she was wheeled into the hospice lounge for the first time, she looked around her at the other patients. Her eyes shone; 'Such material!' she said.

There are some important points to note about hospice care:

- Hospices offer state of the art medical care. Their aim is to minimize discomfort and help the dying and their families
- Those who receive hospice care do not necessarily die sooner than those who remain in hospital
- Providing people with pain relief does not in itself cause death
- Hospice care is designed to help those who are dying to live as fully as possible

Hospital

For the elderly who remain in hospital, intensive medical care is provided at all levels. However, much may seem impersonal and unfamiliar. Nonetheless, there are a number of things that can be done to improve the situation:

- Make sure that the elderly person's living will and other directives are filed in the medical records. Nurses should be informed of them and be prepared to follow their instructions. This is something you will need to check and remind the staff of regularly (see below)
- Visit the hospital as often as possible. It is important to monitor care closely
- Try to ensure that the person receives full medical care
- Make contact with the hospital social worker or chaplain
- Encourage visitors but make sure the visits do not last too long
- Make sure the person is getting as much pain relief as necessary
- Ask nurses if family members are able to spend the night

Anthony had been ill for a very long time. He was ninety-three and had already had two major strokes. As a doctor himself, he was very aware of medical matters. Many years before, he and his wife had signed living wills giving instructions that he was not to be resuscitated. When he went into the hospital after his second stroke, he was very diminished. His memory had disappeared; he was incontinent; he could barely speak and he was plainly unhappy. One morning, when visiting, the family discovered that he had had another episode in the night. The nurse told them that they had nearly lost him, but that there was a young doctor on the spot and all the hospital facilities had been used to revive him. The family were appalled. They pointed out that Anthony had made a living will and the hospital had been clearly informed of this fact. There had been an administrative blunder. Someone down the line had failed to write a 'Do not resuscitate' notice on Anthony's bed.

Anthony lived for another three months in a condition that no one would have wished on anyone.

Options

There are various options that are open to families:

- **Life support.** This commonly refers to a ventilator (respirator) which forces oxygen into the lunges through a tube that is inserted into the nose or mouth
- **Pulling the plug.** This refers to the removal of life support
- **DNR.** This refers to an agreement not to resuscitate the patient if the person's breathing or heart stops
- **CPR.** Cardiopulmonary resuscitation. This is performed when a person's heart or lungs stop working
- Artificial hydration and nutrition

It is helpful to everyone if the family is entirely clear what sort of resuscitation is acceptable and informs the hospital of the fact.

Edie's husband was ninety-two. He had had a stroke and was very incapacitated. His heart was also beating unevenly and when he tried to get up, he tended to fall. In order to prevent possible fractures, the doctors suggested fitting a pacemaker to regulate his heartbeat. Edie hesitated. Many years previously they had both signed living wills and had agreed that they wanted palliative care at the end, and no artificial prolonging of life. Eventually, however, she agreed. The thought of him breaking arms and legs at this stage was intolerable.

Then she began to get confused. It was clear that she had Alzheimer's disease and would need a lot of care herself, but mercifully, in her case, the disease was slow. Edie's husband continued to live on. He probably had several other little strokes. He was not conscious of what was going on around him and he no longer recognized Edie. One day she said innocently to her son who was visiting, 'I gave permission for him to have that pacemaker put in. Now I'm going to give permission for them to take it out!'

After death

Once a person has died, it is necessary to deal with the practical details of the funeral. The first step is to contact a funeral director who will organize details. You will also need to decide about costs. If this is to be done from a distance, it is possible to find the names of funeral homes on the internet. It is best to meet with the funeral directors in their offices. In general they are very experienced and professional and will make it as easy as possible. If you are planning to have a religious service, the funeral director will be able to make suggestions how it can be arranged. When meeting with the clergy who will officiate, you should provide a resume of the person's life and any other information that is needed. This will be necessary even if the clergy knew the deceased well.

If you are writing an obituary for the local or national newspapers, you should include the name of the person who died, his or her date of birth, education, and work experience, membership of organizations, awards, hobbies, and the names of family members. The obituary should include the time and place of a funeral or memorial service and the name of any charity to which donations may be sent. It is useful to include a photograph as well. The obituary should be sent to alumni magazines as well as to the newspapers.

If the person who died had specific wishes regarding how his or her body is to handled, this should be honoured. If not, a decision should be made about what the family prefers. If the intention of the deceased differs from the family, it should be recognized that the funeral is intended for the survivors and this must be an important consideration. There are a number of ways of dealing with the body:

- **Autopsy.** This is an examination of the body performed by a coroner, medical examiner, or physician when the death is unnatural or suspicious. Autopsies can also take place if such an examination is helpful for medical research
- **Organ donation.** Some individuals specify that they wish to

donate organs, such as kidneys or retinas to others
- **Interment.** The body is placed in a casket and buried in a cemetery or graveyard
- **Entombment.** The casket is placed in a mausoleum
- **Cremation.** The body is placed in a box and put into a crematory furnace. Subsequently the ashes are scattered or buried

Esther and Sam had been married for more than sixty years. Esther had always been religious. She left instructions that when she died she wished to be buried with Sam in a Jewish cemetery. However, Sam was the first to go. It was a surprise to everyone when his will was read. He insisted that he wanted to be cremated with no religious service and his ashes scattered in the open air. Since cremation is against Jewish law and ashes cannot be buried in an Orthodox Jewish cemetery, it looked as if Esther and Sam would not lie together in death.

In the event, Esther lived until she was over a hundred. By the time she died there was no one left to go to her funeral except her only son and his wife. Esther had been a devoted wife and they did not like the idea of the two old people being apart. She had always loved nature and they remembered her saying that the woods are God's cathedral. After much discussion they decided that the best thing would be for Esther's body also to be cremated and then they would both go on a quiet trip together to scatter the ashes of both parents in the woods fifty miles from the city. It was a beautiful afternoon and the son felt, when he had finished, that he had done the best he could for his parents.

The following is a list of things that will need to be done:

- Notify those who need to know about the death
- Select a funeral director
- Decide the date of the funeral
- Write an obituary

- Decide whether the body will be buried or cremated
- See if there is a family plot
- Decide whether a graveside service is preferable
- Choose the person who is to officiate at the service
- Select the music
- Decide what kinds of flowers, candles, and guest books will be used
- Ask individuals to serve as pallbearers and ushers
- If there is to be a graveside service, decide whether the casket or urn will be lowered into the grave
- Ask a neighbour who will not be at the service to keep an eye on the house of the person who has died
- Decide whether there will be a gathering after the service and who should be invited
- Organize a programme for the service
- Make arrangements for out of town visitors
- Select a gravestone

Wills

It is important to discover if the person who died has a will. You should:

- Contact relevant parties such as the lawyer, financial planner, and accountant as well as relatives
- Locate the will
- Check with the probate clerk's office
- Contact the person's bank to close accounts and see if there is a safe-deposit box
- Register the death and obtain copies of the death certificate
- Find the person's marriage certificate
- Notify insurance companies
- Contact former employers to see if their pension benefits continue to apply

- Make a list of assets
- List all debts
- Find a copy of the income tax return
- Revise the will of a spouse who is still living

Estate

Most wills specify that the estate will go to the spouse or be divided equally among the children. This can be done with money, but not with personal property. Generally an executor is appointed to organize the distribution. The executor may be a lawyer, but is generally a family member. It is the responsibility of family to divide up personal belongings. This will require care and consideration. It is all too easy for someone to become upset and offended at this point.

- If possible, family members should wait until the grief has subsided before personal property is handed out
- Assign value to each item so everyone can assess its worth. It might be necessary to hire an appraiser. It is important that no one feels they are losing out
- Each family member should decide which items he or she wants, but compromises will have to be made
- Ask an outsider to monitor the division of property
- Decide who will be present when items are to be distributed For the sake of family peace, it might be sensible that the spouses of family members are left at home
- For those who are unable to be present, photographs of items should be provided
- After having sorted through the most valuable items, all other items should be distributed
- If the beneficiaries are unable to agree, the executor should make the final decision

Maud died at the age of eighty-eight. She had been a rich woman and she left a houseful of beautiful things. After the funeral all four sons and their wives descended on the house to organize the final distribution. The youngest son was a lawyer. A scrupulously fair man, he had had everything appraised and he tried to give everyone a fair share. However the bad feeling was unbelievable. At the end of the afternoon everyone was exhausted and it took another twenty years before everyone was on speaking terms again.

The death of a parent evokes many feelings. There may be grief at the loss of the loved one; there may be guilt that not enough was done; there may be relief that the whole difficult process is over. These ambivalences are natural. There are other more complicated feelings. With the death of a parent, children have to face up to the fact that they are now orphans. There is perhaps no one now alive who remembers them as children. No longer are they infants, or adolescents or even young people. They are now irrevocably part of the older generation. Indeed, all too soon, they too will be old.

Afterword

So what do you do if your parents live for ever? Over the years of caring for aged parents, we have formulated ten commandments which have helped us. They are not in any particular order:

1) Respect your parents' independence as long as you can
2) Don't quarrel with your siblings
3) Try not to feel guilty
4) Never depend on a future inheritance
5) Establish a good relationship with carers
6) Be guided by your sense of duty
7) Be realistic about your own feelings
8) Be patient with disabilities
9) Forgive the past
10) Do the very best you can

O

is a symbol of the world,
of oneness and unity. O Books
explores the many paths of whole-
ness and spiritual understanding which
different traditions have developed down
the ages. It aims to bring this knowledge in
accessible form, to a general readership, providing practical spirituality to today's seekers.

For the full list of over 200 titles covering:
ACADEMIC/THEOLOGY • ANGELS • ASTROLOGY/
NUMEROLOGY • BIOGRAPHY/AUTOBIOGRAPHY
• BUDDHISM/ENLIGHTENMENT • BUSINESS/LEADERSHIP/
WISDOM • CELTIC/DRUID/PAGAN • CHANNELLING
• CHRISTIANITY; EARLY • CHRISTIANITY; TRADITIONAL
• CHRISTIANITY; PROGRESSIVE • CHRISTIANITY;
DEVOTIONAL • CHILDREN'S SPIRITUALITY • CHILDREN'S
BIBLE STORIES • CHILDREN'S BOARD/NOVELTY • CREATIVE
SPIRITUALITY • CURRENT AFFAIRS/RELIGIOUS • ECONOMY/
POLITICS/SUSTAINABILITY • ENVIRONMENT/EARTH
• FICTION • GODDESS/FEMININE • HEALTH/FITNESS
• HEALING/REIKI • HINDUISM/ADVAITA/VEDANTA
• HISTORY/ARCHAEOLOGY • HOLISTIC SPIRITUALITY
• INTERFAITH/ECUMENICAL • ISLAM/SUFISM
• JUDAISM/CHRISTIANITY • MEDITATION/PRAYER
• MYSTERY/PARANORMAL • MYSTICISM • MYTHS
• POETRY • RELATIONSHIPS/LOVE • RELIGION/
PHILOSOPHY • SCHOOL TITLES • SCIENCE/
RELIGION • SELF-HELP/PSYCHOLOGY
• SPIRITUAL SEARCH • WORLD
RELIGIONS/SCRIPTURES • YOGA

**Please visit our website,
www.O-books.net**